REPORT WRITING SKILLS

Roy Jeffs

Oliver & Boyd

To Eidda

Oliver & Boyd
Longman House
Burnt Mill
Harlow
Essex CM20 2JE

An Imprint of Longman Group Ltd

© Oliver & Boyd 1990

First published 1990

ISBN 0 05 004482 6

Typeset on Apple Macintosh SE/30 in Palatino 10/13pt.

Produced by Longman Group (F.E.) Ltd
Printed in Hong Kong

Contents

TO THE STUDENT

The aim of this book is to help you to acquire and develop skills as a writer of reports. These skills are not only a vital part of today's English and Communication courses in schools and colleges but are becoming increasingly important in professional life.

As you can see, the book is divided into three main sections. Section One shows you how to plan a report stage by stage from the initial analysis of data through to the first written draft. In Section Two a programme of Guided Activities enables you to practise this sequence of planning and writing stages by tackling a wide variety of report exercises. Section Three deals with the language of reports; it can be studied selectively as an accompaniment to the Guided Activities or as a unit after all or most of the Activities have been completed. At the end of the book a Glossary offers quick reference to the terms used in connection with report writing.

INTRODUCTION

What is a Report?

The Glossary at the end of this book begins its definition of a report as 'a formally written account'. Business letters, legal documents, editorials in 'quality' newspapers and witnesses' statements are other examples of formal writing, so how does a report differ from any of these?

Probably the best way to answer this question is to consider in what way people are helped by reading reports. They may, for instance, decide to carry out a number of recommendations after reading a report on road safety made by a specially appointed committee; or they may gain a better understanding of environmental problems after reading an informative report on the 'greenhouse effect'. As a result of being informed or advised or instructed the reader of a report normally sees a practical application of the material it contains.

In other words, a report is a kind of functional or 'transactional' writing. It can also be described as 'directed' writing. This means that the writers of reports are not free to make an open-ended composition out of their material but are directed by clear 'terms of reference'. They need to produce an account that serves a practical, pre-arranged purpose, often designed by the person calling for the report. These terms of reference form a framework of instructions or guidelines, which control the planning and writing of the report and need to be made explicit to the reader. Two reports might be based on a similar set of data but differ in their selection of material from these data because their terms of reference are different. For example, one writer might make use of information about fox-hunting customs to illustrate a report on rural traditions, while someone else might use the same material for a report on fox-hunting as a barbaric practice to be opposed.

The characteristics of a report – formal style, practical application and control by terms of reference – are summed up in the complete definition which you can find in the Glossary. Reports vary in length from the relatively short accounts in this book to publications of several hundred pages, and they also vary in the purposes they serve. Their essential features, nevertheless, remain the same.

SECTION ONE

Planning Reports: a Step-by-Step Guide

When you are asked to write a report, you need to form a clear picture of what your report is about, who is supposed to be reading it, and why it has to be written. This clear picture can be gained only through careful planning of the task, planning that identifies from the instructions and data everything that is relevant to the report you have to produce.

The following step-by-step guide to planning a report will help you to lay the foundations for your work on the Activity Units in the next section of the book.

Report Planning Guide

Step One

Make a close study of the 'report situation': the instructions you are given, background details, items of information, statistics, diagrams, etc. Check that everything has been seen.

Step Two

Make a **planning checklist** based on these questions:
What is the topic of this report?
What role am I asked to play as a report writer?
Who is supposed to read the report?
What is the purpose of the report?

Step Three

Get an overall idea, or **overview**, of the main sections of the report. This is often supplied in your instructions.

Step Four

Using your planning checklist, select and note down all the **relevant points** required for the main sections.

Step Five

With your overview in mind, **re-order** your chosen relevant points in the way you think best.

Step Six

Remembering the purpose of your report, decide which of the relevant points you should **summarise** into a more concise form and which ones you should **expand** into a more developed version.

Step Seven

Decide which **tone** of writing is most suitable for your report. This will help to establish the right relationship with your reader or readers, as well as to communicate the purpose of the report.

Step Eight

Compose a suitable **introduction and conclusion**. Prepare to write your report.

At first glance this guide might make the planning of reports seem an elaborate and time-consuming process, particularly when most reports have to be written against the clock. You will find, however, that once you have become familiar with the sequence of planning steps they will become an automatic part of report writing. They will actually save you time because your thinking will be immediately directed to the things that matter.

The Planning Guide in Practice

Study the following 'report situation'.

You are a reporter for a weekly community newspaper which is delivered free to all homes in the area. Your editor wants a report on charitable fund-raising activities among groups of people within the community. Your editor's suggestion is that you plan your report along the following lines:

a) Fund-raising as an activity
b) Examples of fund-raising in the area
c) Suggestions for widening community involvement

Write your report in formal continuous prose in 350–400 words. Supply a suitable heading if you wish, and base your material on the following items which you have gathered during your research.

ITEM 1: **Letter from a children's home to Burnside Youth Club** (copy given to you during a visit to the club)

Dear Club Members,

I'm writing to thank you for the generous donation you made to us from the proceeds of your summer fair. We took the children along and were able to appreciate at first hand the tremendous work you all put in to make the occasion a success – in spite of the poor weather! There was something for everyone and everyone in Burnside seemed to be there.

You will be interested to know that, thanks to the generosity of your youth club and other local organisations, our target fund has been reached and we can now go ahead with our plans to purchase a mini-bus. You have played a very important part in enhancing the quality of our children's lives.

Yours sincerely,

John Hampton, Warden.

ITEM 2: **Interview with Andrea Sharp,** organiser of Voluntary Action Burnside

We act as a kind of job-centre for people wanting to offer their free services to help disadvantaged men, women and children, to save animals and so on. An important part of our work is to give advice and help with fund-raising for charity. What we've discovered is that this particular activity seems to be more successful if it is fun for the organisers – 'enjoy yourself in helping others'. I'm not saying that fund-raisers don't stand in the pouring rain shaking collecting tins outside supermarkets – that still goes on – but more and more nowadays there will be an activity which is aimed at exciting public interest. Call it a gimmick if you like – but it's usually something that participants and cash-donors alike find worthwhile and entertaining.

Take sponsoring, for example. Say you want to raise money to buy special sports equipment for disabled people and you have a cash target. Well your group (office-workers, students, taxi-drivers?) gets together to decide what form of sponsorship would work best, how you're going to get publicity, and where and when your event will happen. Apart from fun, the whole thing revolves around challenge: the fund-giver is persuaded into challenging the fund-raiser into achieving something – swimming so many lengths, playing in a musical marathon, or whatever – and when proof of performance is produced the giver stumps up the agreed sum of money. And at the end of the day there's often a real sense of fulfilment for the performers who feel they have gone beyond what were believed to be their personal limits.

ITEM 3: **Extract from** *Working For Free* **by Philip Neale,** a book on voluntary work and fund-raising

The term 'charity' until recently has had unfortunate connotations for many people. The saying 'cold as charity' implies a distance between the consciously generous donor and the 'deserving case' who is left in no doubt about the need to be grateful in return. In recent years, however, this Victorian attitude has given way to a more genuinely caring approach, a more natural community spirit which involves young and old alike. Today a benefactor might be a youngster raising cash for an old people's home by washing customers' vehicles in a supermarket car park; or it might be a licensee who donates the proceeds of a raffle in his public house to the children's ward of the local hospital.

In helping to bring about this close identification between giver and recipient the most powerful allies of any charitable organisation are undoubtedly the mass media. Consider the potency of television: millions of pounds are raised in forty-eight hours during the annual 'Children in Need' appeal; massive amounts of cash are generated after viewers have seen pictures of earthquake victims. Television, radio, magazines, newspapers, the record industry – they all stir the public's compassion and imagination, and hence generosity. The results are often spectacular because the benefits are seen by all to be practical: it is simply common-sense to give what one can easily spare to those whose need is so acute...

In the community there are two dimensions of fund-raising: the local dimension and the nationwide or world-wide dimension. The former involves groups of people raising money for local institutions or concerns or individuals. The targets are usually specific – new premises for a first-aid organisation, Christmas presents for single-parent families, provision and training of guide-dogs for the blind, and so on. As long as the need is clearly advertised the public response is usually forthcoming, particularly when a spirit of neighbourliness is stimulated. The wider dimension of fund-raising makes use of local agencies, such as Oxfam shops run by voluntary helpers, and individuals or groups who collect money through various means including traditional collecting-tin methods on 'flag days' and the like. In these cases the response levels are generally high because the charities are so well known – even seasonal (poppy day, for instance) – that people automatically reach for their purses and dip into their pockets.

ITEM 4: **Digest of interview with pupils from local secondary school**

It's amazing what you can do when you set your mind to it ... Last winter some of us were working in our school's community involvement programme and we were really shocked, you know, by the conditions some old people had to live in during the cold weather ... Anyway, we worked out what was needed ... In most cases it was practical help like improving draught-proofing round doors and windows, buying safe mobile heaters, thermal clothing – that sort of thing ... So we got together with some of the teachers to organise a 'Beat the Cold' week to raise money for all this. The school band did a charity concert, we had a sale of work, the seniors put on a fashion show – even the first-year kids did their bit with a sponsored silence! All in all it was a great success. Apart from the money we raised it really made everyone think about a problem that doesn't normally occur to us, because the whole week was focused on this one cause.

ITEM 5: **Editor's memo**

Re your article on fund-raising

Suggest you emphasise that everyone can do this, not just the professionals. All groups are potential fund-raisers. Mention our weekly spotlight on fund-raising in area (starting in two months).

We can plan the writing of the report in this way.

Step One: *'Report situation'*

350–400 word report for community newspaper on fund-raising for charity in Burnside area. Items: letter from children's home to youth club; interview with organiser of 'Voluntary Action'; extract from book on subject; interview with pupils; editor's memo.

Step Two: *Planning checklist*

Topic? Charity fund-raising activities in Burnside area.

Role? Community newspaper reporter.

Readers? People living in community served by newspaper.

Purpose? i) to provide information about forms & examples of fund-raising in Burnside;

ii) to encourage more people to participate in fund-raising.

Step Three: *Overview of main sections*

a) (Introduction)

Fund-raising as an activity

b) Examples of fund-raising in the Burnside area

c) Suggestions for widening community involvement

(Conclusion)

Step Four: *Selection of relevant points*

(N.B. the choice and combination of these will be a matter for individual judgment, and the following are offered for suggestion.)

ITEM 1 1.1 Burnside Youth Club organised summer fair to raise money for children's home mini-bus. Quality of children's lives improved.

ITEM 2 2.1 'Voluntary Action' help with fund-raising for charity.

2.2 The more fun for organisers, the more successful the activity – 'enjoy yourself in helping others'.

2.3 At heart of enterprise an activity aimed at exciting public interest (gimmick?) – worthwhile & entertaining.

2.4 Sponsoring: group decides form, publicity, where & when.

2.5 Revolves around challenge. Sense of fulfilment for person sponsored.

ITEM 3　　3.1 Unfortunate connotations of word 'charity' – distance between donor and 'deserving case'.

3.2 Today different: natural community spirit among young & old. All kinds of benefactors.

3.3 Powerful help of mass media, especially TV (appeals). Media stir public generosity. Spectacular results – people see it as common-sense to give to needy.

3.4 Two dimensions of fund-raising:
1) local – group raise money for locally based, specific targets: spirit of neighbourliness from clearly advertised need;
2) wider – local agencies (e.g. Oxfam shops) & groups/individuals (e.g. flag-days): charities well-known, so high response levels.

ITEM 4　　4.1 Orr Bridge High School pupils in community involvement programme – shocked by cold weather conditions some old people had to live in. Decided practical help needed.

4.2 'Beat the Cold' week fund-raising campaign (e.g.s of activities).

4.3 Success in raising money and increasing awareness by focus on one cause.

ITEM 5　　5.1 Emphasise how virtually anyone can become involved

5.2 Persuade readers to consider fund-raising potential of groups they belong to.

5.3 Mention paper's forthcoming weekly spotlight on fund-raising.

Step Five: Re-ordering of relevant points according to overview

a)　Introduction / fund-raising as an activity.

a(i)　Old view of 'charity' contrasted with natural community spirit of today: benefactors of all kinds & age groups (3.1, 3.2, 5.1).

a(ii)　Fun for organisers: excite public interest (2.1, 2.2, 2.3).

a(iii) Sponsoring as a major form: concept of challenge (2.4, 2.5).

b)　Examples of fund-raising in Burnside area.

b(i)　2 dimensions – wider & local (3.4) (N.B. reversed order).

b(ii)　E.g.s of local initiatives: Burnside Youth Club's summer fair (1.1) & Orr Bridge's 'Beat the Cold' week (4.1, 4.2, 4.3).

c)　Suggestions for widening community involvement / Conclusion.

c(i)　Responding to mass media: individual or group action (3.3).

c(ii)　Persuade readers to consider fund-raising potential of groups (5.2).

c(iii) Mention forthcoming weekly spotlight (5.3).

Step Six: Summary and Expansion of relevant points

(N.B. most of the points in Items 1 to 4 will be summarised (with some illustrative examples included where appropriate), while points in Item 5 will tend to be expanded. In some reports the amount of expanded material in relation to summarised points will be greater. Much depends on the judgment of the writer.)

See final version.

Step Seven: Choice of tone

A quick review of your planning checklist will help you to establish the right tone for your report. In this case, it should not be completely detailed although a fairly impersonal tone is appropriate to the reporter's role and relationship with a wide readership. Because the report is intended to persuade as well as inform a sense of commitment should be conveyed, particularly in the final section of the report. The writer and readers live in the same community and share similar concerns.

Step Eight: Introduction and Conclusion

Starting and finishing reports are difficult for report writers, particularly if there is no clear guidance in the instructions. In this case the overview of main sections offers some help, and this is reinfored by our choice of an appropriate tone (i.e. persuasion at the end). In the final version you will note that the introduction makes use of the 'old and new' contrast as a way of catching the reader's attention, and the conclusion is designed to whet the reader's interest in the forthcoming weekly spotlight.

This is what the final version might look like.

```
                    ENJOY HELPING OTHERS
There was a time when 'charity' created a wide gap between the
generous giver and the grateful 'deserving case'. Today it is
different, as Philip Neale reminds us in his book, "Working for
Free". Fund-raising for charity nowadays is much more of a
genuine activity, part of a natural community spirit involving
all kinds of people of all ages.

    Andrea Sharp's group, Voluntary Action Burnside, shows the
way by helping people to help others, particularly by raising
funds. She emphasises that the organisers' enjoyment is vital
to the success of a fund-raising activity because this enjoyment
underpins their ability to excite public interest in worthwhile
and entertaining events. Sponsored activities combine this
sense of fun with the stimulus of challenge. The result is that
performers can have a sense of fulfilment in their achievements
as well as helping good causes.
```

Sponsoring is only one example of Burnside's fund-raising enterprises. There are local agencies of national organisations, such as Oxfam shops, and people also respond generously to flag-days because they immediately recognise famous charities. There is also what Philip Neale calls the local dimension of fund-raising, where people work as teams to reach specific local targets, appealing to a spirit of neighbourliness. Here, Burnside Youth Club organised a summer fair to purchase a mini-bus for a children's home, thus helping to enhance the quality of the children's lives. Under the title of 'Beat the Cold Week', Orr Bridge High School organised events ranging from a fashion show to a sponsored silence, in order to raise money to improve heating and insulation in the homes of elderly people.

Initiatives like these are examples to us all. We have seen the spectacular success of television appeals for public donations and we can continue to respond, but there is more that we can do. It is not only professional organisers who can run appeals: every single one of us is capable of becoming involved in raising money for good causes. Nearly all our readers belong to one group or another, be it at work, school or college, or be it a sporting, social or recreational group. Whatever its nature, it could be seen as a potential fund-raising organisation.

To promote this, our newspaper is launching a weekly spotlight on fund-raising in Burnside. It starts two months from now. Will you be part of it?

388 words (N.B. 'fund-raising' counts as one word.)

POINTS TO NOTICE

1. The above is a suggested version and is not offered as a model to be imitated. Although there should be a broad consensus on which items of material should be selected and which ideas should be emphasised, there is still considerable scope for individual judgment with regard to the final presentation of the report. There are different ways of being right.

2. Some substitutions have been made (for example, 'gap' for 'distance') but it is not necessary to translate all the original wording of items into your own. Phrases such as 'worthwhile and entertaining', 'spirit of neighbourliness' and 'local dimension' appear in the final version in their original form because they are key expressions and there is little point in changing them. Note, however, that two of the contributors of the material are acknowledged.

3. Linking expressions, such as 'shows the way by', 'the result is that', 'is only one example', 'Here, ... ', and 'To promote this', are used to relate the various selected points, thus providing coherence in the report. (Section Three deals with this aspect in detail.)

4. The tone of the report is formal, but sufficiently relaxed to allow a mildly

persuasive note to emerge in the last two paragraphs without affecting its consistency. This reflects the writer's sense of commitment as indicated in the terms of reference; note, for instance, the use of 'us', 'we', 'there is more that we can do', and 'examples to us all'. The question which ends the report may therefore be interpreted as an invitation rather than a peremptory demand.

Now see if you can write your own version of the report on fund-raising. You are free to select whatever points you consider to be relevant and to re-organise them as you think fit. You may decide to wait until you have practised some of the Activity Units in the next Section.

SECTION TWO

Activity Units

Activity Unit One

FOCUS OF STUDY:
Planning Guide – Steps One, Two and Three

the 'Report Situation'
the Checklist
the Overview of main sections

GUIDED ACTIVITY

In this Unit we are going to concentrate on the three preliminary steps of building up a clear picture of what the report is dealing with, who it is for, and why it is being written. In practice, you would not normally write anything down at this stage: the questions at the end of the Unit are there to help you identify the points you need to know in order to complete the remaining steps of the planning guide.

REPORT ON LOCAL ATTRACTIONS AND PLACES OF INTEREST
FOR OVERSEAS VISITORS

You are a tutor in a summer school which teaches English to young people from a number of different countries. During their courses at the school, they stay with families in the town of Hestonbury, where the school is based. The Director of the school has asked you to provide a report on local attractions in Hestonbury, and places of interest in and around the town, which would appeal to your students (whose ages range from twelve to nineteen). Your report will form part of a package of publicity material which the school will send to various organisations abroad.

Write the report in about 350 words, basing your material on the items of information which follow. It is suggested that you organise your report around these sections:

a) brief introduction to the town of Hestonbury
b) places of interest for visitors in the town and its surrounding areas
c) entertainment, sports and leisure centres
d) concluding comments

The style in which your report is written should be formal but fairly relaxed: you are aiming to provide a concise outline of what Hestonbury has to offer in cultural and recreational terms.

ITEM 1: Extract from Official Tourists' Guide to Hestonbury

Remains of a Roman settlement were excavated during the 1950s on a site north of the River Taire, and fine specimens are to be found in the local museum. The medieval castle, partly ruined, offers splendid views to the harbour, Seal Island and the open sea. (One hour motor-launch trips round the island can be booked during May to September.) ... On Wednesdays the covered weekly market offers household bargains as well as a wide range of traditional craftware, while in the jewellers' shops along the ancient Goldsmiths' Gate you can order local gemstones to be made into jewellery and ornaments of your chosen design... The summer festival is a must for visitors: its variety of dramatic, musical and artistic performances rivals those of larger towns and cities... The famous Victorian Village is only forty-five minutes away by coach.

ITEM 2: Publicity leaflet from the Hestonbury Playhouse

This year's Summer Season of plays and musicals provides a mixture of old favourites and new surprises.

There's more than a whiff of sea air in Gilbert and Sullivan's *H.M.S. Pinafore* (first two weeks of July), while our very own playwright Susan Stokes takes a wry look at the world of fashion in her comedy *Hemline* which runs from 16 to 20 July.

We close the first month and enter August with a new surprise package of magic, clowning and 'opportunity knocks' shows for young hopefuls in 'Summer Cavalcade' – all produced by the Hestonbury Young People's Theatre. Come along and be a part of it, or just watch if you prefer – it's open to everyone!

Our action-packed season ends with a colourful revival of that ever-popular musical *Fiddler on the Roof* (13 to 18 August).

See you there!

ITEM 3: Your own notes after discussion with Director

Emphasis must be on wide range of low-cost attractions that appeal to the age-groups of our students – last year quite a few of the younger ones had to send home for more money. The new Disco will be a firm favourite but must tactfully suggest a bit of chaperoning by group leaders (without of course implying that Hestonbury has gangs of yobs roaming the streets). Summer exhibitions at the Art Gallery and Museum look good – and they're free! Glad to note that enough tutors have volunteered to act as guides on the introductory coach tours around the town (we can take in the Haunted Bakery now that it's been restored). Scheduled excursions along the coast and to nearby tourist spots have usual students' discounts this summer. Director stresses 'Culture': that's important, but so are the informal things - e.g. 'olde worlde' shops, open-air cafe near the castle where everyone meets everyone else. And we <u>are</u> actually a friendly lot! Must mention the short-season bus passes for students to get about the town cheaply. If we get students' names before they arrive here we can make early applications on their behalf and have the passes ready before they start their courses.

ITEM 4: **Extract from local newspaper article**

NEW SPORTS COMPLEX FOR HESTONBURY

...After opening the Complex, Councillor Prentiss paid tribute to the dedicated efforts of fund-raisers and campaigners in creating what she called "a magnet for all sports-minded and keep-fit enthusiasts" in the area. She hoped, too, that there would be many like herself who, though not necessarily 'sporty types', would nonetheless be enticed by the excellent facilities of the Complex to participate in at least one of its many activities. These ranged, she was assured, "from martial arts to country dancing, from yoga to water polo".

In addition to the three floors of sports halls, a swimming pool and specialist areas, the Complex offers a cafeteria with a strong accent on health-foods and a large conference-suite with audio-visual facilities...

Questions

1   Analyse the 'report situation' – your instructions and items of information. What is the general picture?

2   Go on to draw up a planning checklist. Write down your answers to the following:
    What is the topic of this report?
    What is the writer's role?
    Who is supposed to read the report?*
    What is the purpose of the report?
    (*Apart from the Director)

3   Look at the suggested division of the report into main sections. Get an *overview* of these sections by quickly matching them with material from the instructions and items of material. On what material would you base your 'concluding comments'?

4   Do you foresee any problems in adapting the material either in its content or in its style of presentation to the purpose your report must serve? Discuss this matter with other students.

We shall return to the 'Hestonbury' report in order to carry out Steps Four and Five in the next Activity Unit. For the moment you might find it helpful to practise Steps One, Two and Three of the planning guide by glancing through the instructions and items of material in some of the report exercises in later Activity Units.

Activity Unit Two

FOCUS OF STUDY: Planning Guide – Steps Four and Five

selection of relevant points
re-ordering of relevant points

GUIDED ACTIVITY

In Activity Unit One you were shown how to identify the requirements of your report writing task. You did this by assessing the 'report situation', compiling a planning checklist and taking an overview of the main sections of the report.

Your next two steps involve making two closely related decisions: which of the many items of information (or data) you should select as relevant to the checklist (task, role, readership and purpose); and how you should re-order these relevant points in the most effective way. More often than not, the selection process will require considerable 'pruning', and you should remember that there is as much skill in deciding what to leave out as in deciding what to include. You will also find that the order of selected points suggested by your checklist and overview will differ substantially from the original one.

Re-read the instructions and items relating to the 'Hestonbury' exercise in Activity Unit One. Use the notes you made to help you in answering the following questions.

Questions

1   Look over the suggested approach to Steps Four and Five of the Planning Guide in Practice in Section One of this book (pages 10 and 11).

2   Using this approach, which points would you select from the four items of information as relevant to your task? Write them in note form.

3   With your overview in mind, how would you re-order these points in the most effective way? Write them down in the suggested form.

4   How does your version compare with those of other people?

5   Now try, as a preliminary exercise, a first draft of a report on Hestonbury as required in the instructions in Activity Unit One. When you have completed the remaining Activity Units, re-read this draft before attempting a final version.

Activity Unit Three

FOCUS OF STUDY: Planning Guide – Step Six

Summary of relevant points and expansion of relevant points

GUIDED ACTIVITY

By now you have almost certainly discovered that even though the points you have selected for your report are relevant to the task they are often too wordy to be included in their original form. In some cases, however, it is the opposite: some points are expressed too briefly and need to be 'fleshed out' or expanded to make the message clear. In any case, a report reads and sounds better if it is written in the reporter's own words (no matter how firmly based on the original data) and in order to achieve this you should master the complementary skills of summary and expansion.

Study the following example.

REPORT ON 'UNFAIR DISMISSAL'

Read the following items. Then write a report in formal, continuous prose on the subject of claims by employees against their employers on the grounds of unfair dismissal.

You should, in your report:

(a) introduce the topic of 'unfair dismissal', briefly explaining what it means;

(b) Illustrate, by reference to relevant data, the issues that are often dealt with by industrial tribunals when considering cases of unfair dismissal claims;

(c) Provide a suitable conclusion.

You are not being asked to state your personal opinion on the subject of unfair dismissal but to provide an unbiased report based entirely on your selection of information and conclusions contained in the items. Your report should be approximately 350 to 400 words in length.

SACKED: THE SUPER-SALESMAN WHO BROKE THE RULES

COLIN ANDERSON's luxury sports-car sales record was second to none, according to his bosses at Northern Garages Ltd. Indeed, his efforts had helped to push the firm's profits to a new high last year, earning him the title Salesperson of the Year for the second time running.

But yesterday, at a Bridgeton industrial tribunal, Anderson lost his claim for unfair dismissal by Northern Garages.

Northern personnel manager, Mr Steven Craig, claimed that Mr Anderson's sales techniques had already brought him some serious warnings because of his refusal to follow certain company procedures. And last April, in deliberate contravention of a management rule, Mr Anderson allowed a potential customer to test-drive a £23,000 sports-car unaccompanied and without any precautionary checks on the customer's credentials. The sports-car was later found abondoned, "a complete wreck", over a hundred miles away from the garage salesroom.

In spite of Mr Anderson's claim that he had responded to the customer's "considerable persuasive powers" in allowing him to test-drive the car and that, as a salesman with a reputation to keep, he was under great pressure from the company to meet sales targets, the tribunal found Northern Garages had acted reasonably in treating the applicant's conduct as a sufficient reason for his dismissal.

At the industrial tribunal offices in Deancastle today, Miss Janice Sheringham, a twenty-two-year-old hairdresser, had her claim for unfair dismissal upheld against her former employers, 'Hair-By-Design' of Deancastle.

Miss Sheringham had been dismissed from her hairdressing job last February on the grounds of incapability. It was alleged by the manageress of the firm, Mrs Sheila Gerrard, that on several occasions Miss Sheringham, who had been taken on by the previous manager eighteen months ago, had not only upset customers by failing to carry out their instructions but, in Mrs Gerrard's words, had "reacted defensively and impertinently" to her customers' complaints. In spite of what Mrs Gerrard claimed to be "numerous warnings" Miss Sheringham's incompetence threatened to undermine the firm's reputation and the management was left with no option but dismissal.

For her part, Miss Sheringham claimed Mrs Gerrard had been

opposed to her appointment a year and a half ago. Since taking over as manageress, Mrs Gerrard had allegedly sought every opportunity to harass her into making mistakes over customers' hair, but that in spite of this her mistakes were still "few and far between". She claimed her attitude to customers was courteous and reasonable.

In their judgment, the tribunal found insufficient evidence to support the management's claims against Miss Sheringham. No complaints of incapability had been lodged against her by the previous manager and evidence pointed to the applicant's popularity among regular customers and fellow-employees. The tribunal ordered that Miss Sheringham be reinstated by her employers.

ITEM 3: **Extracts from a government leaflet**

a) Industrial tribunals are independent judicial bodies. They have permanent offices in the larger centres of population and sit in most parts of the country ... Persons (or other bodies) bringing cases to the tribunals are known as applicants and those against whom such cases are brought are known as respondents.

b) What is unfair dismissal?

Dismissal of an employee will be considered fair only if the employer can show the reason for it was one of the following:

a reason related to the employee's capability of qualification for the job;

a reason related to the employee's conduct;

redundancy (i.e. where the employer's need for employees to do certain work has ceased or diminished, or is expected to do so) a statutory duty or restriction on either the employer or the employee which prevents the employment being continued;

some other substantial reason which could justify the dismissal.

c) How does the Tribunal help a successful applicant?

The Industrial Tribunal has three possible remedies for unfair dismissal, two of which involve re-employment of the applicant by the employer:

re-instatement (the employer is to be treated in all respects as though the dismissal had not occurred);

re-engagement (the employee is to be re-employed but not necessarily in the same job or on the same terms and conditions of employment);

compensation award (a sum of money to be determined by the Tribunal).

Questions

1 Carry out Steps One to Five.

2 Check the notes you have made of selected and re-ordered points against the original versions in the items of information. Decide which ones should be written in your first draft as summaries of the original text. Then decide which points should be expanded into a longer version.

3 Write your first draft of the report, incorporating your findings in answer to Question 2.

4 Compare your first draft with other people's versions.

FURTHER PRACTICE

To improve your summarising and expansion skills as a writer, practise with articles in newspapers and magazines, or chapters in text-books and similar publications which interest you. Set yourself an aim in doing this so that your efforts are focused towards something definite.

Activity Unit Four

FOCUS OF STUDY: Planning Guide – Step Seven

Deciding on a suitable tone to establish the right relationship with readers to convey clearly the purpose of the report

GUIDED ACTIVITY

Your report planning has now reached an advanced stage! But before working out your introduction and conclusion you should at this point pause to consider how the *tone* of your report is to be tackled. What do we mean by 'tone' in writing?

In speech, tone is conveyed by variations in sound-qualities: we can say things gently, harshly, sarcastically, solemnly, etc. without necessarily changing vocabulary. A writer, however, must use variations in vocabulary, sentence-form and punctuation to make clear the exact tone of a message. For example, the request 'Will you close that window?' has a less polite tone than 'Would you mind closing that window, please?' or 'You wouldn't mind closing that window, would you?' A writer's selection of tone pinpoints his or her attitude to the subject of the writing and to the person or persons reading it.

The tone of a report should normally be *formal* and *neutral*; that is, it should not include colloquial, conversational or emotive expressions, slang, jargon or regional dialect words. (It is not wrong to use such expressions in themselves, merely inappropriate in a formal piece of writing like a report.) At the same time, you should not confuse formality of tone with pomposity, wordiness or starchiness: aim for straightforward fluency of expression. The tone of BBC news broadcasts is a reasonable guide.

Finally, your tone must be *consistent* throughout the report. The items on which you are asked to base the substance of your reports are often varied in tone (popular journalese, legalistic, casual-conversational, official, and so on), but the resulting report must maintain the same tone throughout. Too many report writers lose marks because they allow the different tones of original items to 'speak through' their reports.

Study the following report, paying particular regard to the variation in style and tone of the different items of material.

EATING FOR HEALTH

You have just attended a one-day conference organised by a group of nutritionists and medical experts in conjunction with the education authority. The conference, which was attended by two hundred students from secondary schools and a college of further education, was held because of a concern to improve the awareness among young people of the importance of nutrition in their lives.

You have been asked to write a report on the issues raised and discussed during the conference. Your readers will be teachers and fellow-students, for the most part non-specialists in the subject but nevertheless interested in the topics which were dealt with. You may wish to develop your report, which should be in 350 to 400 words of formal continuous prose, along the following lines:

a) the purpose of the conference;

b) highlights of talks and group discussions;

c) conclusions you have drawn.

ITEM 1: From the Conference programme

EATING FOR HEALTH

A One-Day Conference for young people in post-compulsory education, Piriefield College.

9.15 am   Welcome, and details of discussion group venues and issue of discussion packs

9.30   Opening Address by Dr Marion Carr, director of Institute for Nutritional Research, University of Westdale.

10.15   Slide presentation on food processing methods

10.45   Refreshments

11.00 am–

3.30 pm   Morning and afternoon group discussions
           (lunch break from 1.00–2.00 pm)

3.30–4.00 Plenary session and closing address.

ITEM 2: Your notes on Opening Address

1. Today's society — wider choice of foods than ever before, seasonal foods always available thanks to modern processing techniques. Food relatively cheaper (average person can have adequate diet on smaller % of budget). We know more about

nutrition. So are we healthier?

2. Answer: not necessarily. Taller, live longer, eradicated many diet-related diseases. But some diseases have increased: high blood pressure & heart disease, diabetes, allergies (or at least we are more aware of them).

3. Problems of modern lifestyle — unbalanced diet (too much of some food, not enough of others) — e.g. too much cholesterol in our blood, too much sugar, not enough fibre, etc.; bad feeding habits — hurried meals, missed meals, unbalanced meals; not enough exercise to utilise benefits of food (less of a problem among young people); harmful additives to food (may cause allergies); poor food preparation & cooking.

4. Aim of conference: help us examine what & how we eat — how lifestyle affects nutrition and nutrition affects lifestyle. Packs of material designed to stimulate discussion (students & food experts in each of the ten groups). Pass on our findings to fellow-students and friends.

ITEM 3: **Extracts from material in Discussion Pack (full pack available for anyone interested.)**

Extract 1 – from newspaper report on dental health:

... The British are now eating a record amount of chocolate and sweets, but our dental health has never been better. And now, for the first time, the major British food companies have joined forces with dentists in a concerted effort to reduce the amount of tooth decay even further... Thanks mainly to fluoride in toothpaste and better dental hygiene, health officials are looking forward to almost eradicating tooth decay by the year 2000. But there is still an enormous amount of work to be done educating the public about oral hygiene and how best to use foods... We have to accept that most foods produce dental caries [decay] and then agree on finding ways to limit these as much as possible... It is commonly held that a tooth would be rotted away in a glass of cola overnight. What is not realised is that entirely natural orange juice would cause the same damage, only quicker. It is the way foods are used which affects decay: 20 boiled sweets eaten with a meal would cause no damage to teeth, but if you ate the same throughout the day there would be problems... Sensible dietary habits, regular dental care and good oral hygiene are the important factors preventing dental caries...

Extract 2 – from booklet on health and lifestyle for young people:

Let's face it, some people seem to look great all the time – without appearing to have to work at it – and others of us are let down by our looks no matter how much attention we pay to skin and hair care. If lotions and potions are having little effect, it could be that you're not watching what's going inside your body!

Daily quota

What we eat and drink affects how we look and that doesn't just mean counting the calories when the inches creep on. To function properly our bodies need a daily intake of a whole range of vitamins and minerals and the best way to provide this is to eat as wide a range of foods as possible every day. If you fill yourself with junk food, day in day out, your body will react – spots, dry skin, sore eyes, dull hair – and you certainly won't be feeling at your best. You may feel tired and irritable even when you've had plenty of sleep. Hamburgers and chips are fine but only if you restrict them to once a week and make sure you're eating properly the rest of the time. Meat, liver, wholemeal flour and bread, cereals, eggs, cheese, milk and leafy green vegetables are all valuable suppliers of the B group of vitamins. This essential group promotes growth, helps protect against infections and also affects how you feel mentally. If you are deficient in these vitamins you may develop cracking at the corners of the mouth, mouth ulcers, a sore tongue, red, greasy skin on the face and patches of rough pimply skin on the upper arms, bottom and thighs.

Citrus sense

The list sounds awful, doesn't it? Mum's advice to 'eat up your greens' certainly makes good sense. And eating carrots for your eyesight isn't far wrong either. Carrots certainly contain valuable vitamin A and if you're short of this your eyes may become bloodshot, dry and gritty and you may develop night blindness which means you can't see objects in the dark. We all know about vitamin C coming from citrus fruits like oranges, lemons and grapefruits but it is also found in potatoes and green vegetables. Lack of vitamin C can cause dandruff and scaly skin, so before you reach out for the anti-dandruff shampoo, make sure your diet isn't faulty. Some teenagers suffer from what used to be called 'growing pains' – aching legs and pains in the knee which seem to have no physical cause. The remedy is to make sure you're eating plenty of fish, liver, margarine and eggs, which all contain vitamin D. We also absorb this from the sunlight so, especially in winter, make sure you get outside in the fresh air when the weather permits. Mind you, fresh air and exercise should be part of your daily routine. As well as helping tone up the body, exercise makes the body work more efficiently and, paradoxically, it makes you feel less hungry so you won't be so tempted to indulge in a bar of chocolate.

Extract 3 – Extract from pamphlet on nutrients

Food can be divided into a number of parts which do different jobs in the body. These parts are called nutrients. All food contains nutrients, but hardly any food contains them all. This means that we need to eat a variety of foods to get all the nutrients we need for good health. Your recipe for good health should contain all the following ingredients, the six nutrients:

1. **Proteins** – these are used for body-building and repair. They are the 'building blocks' of the body.

2. **Starches and sugars (carbohydrates)** – these are used for energy. Think of them as the 'fuel' of your body.

3. **Fats and oils (lipids)** – these are also used for energy and warmth.

4. **Vitamins and mineral salts** – each different vitamin and mineral salt does several different jobs in your body. They help your body to make good use of the other nutrients and protect itself from disease.

5. **Water** – this is the essential liquid in which every body process takes place. A shortage of water is dangerous to health.

6. **Dietary fibre** – this is sometimes called roughage. Dietary fibre is an indigestible material which is not absorbed by the body. It helps the body to dispose of waste material efficiently.

Extract 4 – from pamphlet on food processing and cooking

In most instances the preparation and cooking of food involve some loss of nutrients. Losses may also be caused when foods are dried, washed, or subjected to heat, air or long storage. If food has to be cooked before being eaten then certain losses are inevitable. However, manufacturing processes can often be improved so that the losses are reduced. For example, vacuum-drying and freeze-drying have reduced these losses.

Examples of processing and cooking losses

		Loss
Thiamin		
Canned ham		40%
Roasting and stewing mutton		30%
Peas,	boiling	15%
	canning	60%
	drying and boiling	70%
Potatoes,	boiling	25%
	steaming, baking and frying	10%
Riboflavin		
Peas,	boiling	25%
	canning	50%
	drying and boiling	50%
Potatoes,	boiling	25%
	steaming, baking and frying	no loss

Nicotinic acid

Peas,	boiling	40%
	canning	50%
	drying and boiling	60%
Potatoes,	boiling	30%
	steaming, baking and frying	no loss

Vitamin C

Fruit,	stewing	30–40%
	canning	30–40%
Potatoes,	peeling and boiling	30–50%
	boiling without peeling	20–40%
	baking in skin	20–40%
	frying	25–35%

During winter storage potatoes lose about one-sixth of their vitamin C every month.

It is worth bearing in mind that although the fresh vegetables are somewhat more nutritious and more attractive, the choice is frequently not between preserved foods and fresh foods but between preserved foods and no food at all. Green peas are in season in Britain for only a few weeks and only the preserved ones are available for the rest of the year. Moreover, some 'fresh' foods may be many days old while processed foods are usually frozen or canned immediately after harvesting.

ITEM 4: Your notes on issues discussed by your group

1st reaction shared with others - boring, boring, boring! All know this stuff about vitamins, exercise, etc.

But became really interesting. <u>Balance</u> is the thing - you can include quite a lot (even junk food occasionally) as long as the overall mixture is right. Lot of discussion about exercise - & disagreement about how much needed!

Water is good for you! <u>The</u> vital nutrient said some.

Some vegetarians in group defended animal-free diet: plenty of protein in beans & pulses (iron too), vegetarian cheese, etc. All agreed that consciously leaving out certain foods can make you a better self-taught nutritionist - you have to keep tabs on what you eat to stay healthy.

After lunch (very healthy!) discussed related aspects. Food preparation - surprising facts (e.g. is fresh always best?). Good news about the dentist - but most agreed that this was not a licence to gorge on sweets.

Group conclusion: healthy eating should be seen as vital part of one's whole lifestyle, not just an adjunct to it. We can actually <u>choose</u> to be healthy, at least in our society. (We could feed the world with our surpluses and still be well-nourished - but this is a subject for another conference.)

1   Carry out Planning Steps One to Seven, preparing suitable notes.

2   Re-examine the four items of information in terms of their variation in tone. For example, the formality of extract 1 in Item 3 contrasts with the chatty tone of extract 2 in the same item. Decide on the kind of tone your report will be written in: formal, certainly, but perhaps a little less impersonal than, say, that of Item 3, extract 4? Above all, aim to make your tone consistent right through the report.

3   Write your first draft of the report. Read it out aloud to yourself, if possible, or at least imagine the tone of voice you would hear if it were read aloud. Does it sound appropriate to your readership and purpose? Are there any inconsistencies? Make any alterations that might be necessary.

FURTHER PRACTICE

Judging the right tone for a piece of writing requires considerable practice. You should aim to develop a sensitive 'ear' for subtle variations of informal and formal writing. Extensive reading of a wide range of publications is vital to this acquisition. A useful practice is to compare the tones of two or more versions of a similar topic, such as different newspaper reports of the same item of news.

Activity Unit Five

FOCUS OF STUDY: *Planning Guide – Step Eight*

Composing a suitable introduction and conclusion.

GUIDED ACTIVITY

Now that you have organised the substance of your report (sometimes referred to as the 'body' of the report), and you have decided on a suitable tone, you are ready for the final stage of the plan: the introduction and the conclusion.

A good introductory paragraph does several things. It immediately acquaints the reader with the topic being dealt with; it focuses attention on the purpose of the report (information, recommendation, persuasion, complaint, request, etc.); it strikes up a relationship between reader and writer and establishes the writer's role in compiling the report; and it sets the tone of the whole report. In short, the aim of writing your introduction is to make the best use of the substance of the report.

The form which your conclusion takes depends on how you intend your reader or readers to use the 'message' you have conveyed in the report. In some cases your concluding paragraph may need to be little more than a brief summary of the important points, or possibly a re-emphasis of the purpose that has already been made clear. At other times you may wish to use your last paragraph to add something substantial to the body of the report, such as a decision or a recommendation. In all cases, your conclusion must be firm, concise and clearly indicative of the content and purpose of the report as a whole.

Look at the next report.

CHOOSING THE RIGHT CAMERA: A CONSUMER REPORT

You are a student attending a course in Communication. Next term, your class is to work on an assignment called 'Photography as a medium of communication': it will be divided into two groups of students, each aiming to produce a photographic exhibition at the end of the term. A budget of about £300 has been made available for the purchase of camera equipment (new or second-hand) for the two groups, and your tutor has asked the group-leaders (of whom you are one) to recommend suitable purchases in the form of written reports.

The following items will form the basis of your report, which is to be written in approximately 350 words of formal, continuous prose. In it you should:
a) make clear the purpose of your report;
b) outline the various options for purchase and consider any related factors;
c) make your recommendation.

ITEM 1: **Extract from *'Popular Photography'* magazine.**
... So here then are our top five *BEST BUYS* for the budget-conscious photographer. All value-for-money single lens reflex cameras designed to give impressive results in 35mm photography.

- *REGIUS 750* Still under £100 (just, at £99.50 from most retailers) and good for beginners. But clumsy and heavy to lug about and limited range of shutter speeds (1/30 to 1/500 sec.). You'll need a separate exposure meter.

- *MULTIFLEX AM4* At around £120, this is great value: still heavy and basic but shutter speed range of 1 to 1/1000 sec. and sophisticated built-in metering opens up wide areas of camera-work. Flashgun (£19.50) and zoom lens (£49) complete the outfit for all your photo situations.

- *KROMATIK V-7* They're now offering a complete photographic package (camera body, zoom lens, flash, filters and case) for around £170 – and that's hard to beat. On the bulky side and its oddly positioned controls need careful handling. Same features as Multiflex AM4.

- *ALPHA 3TL* Another package deal – all that the Kromatic offers but with the advantage of completely automatic controls (switched back to manual when preferred). Light, easy to operate yet a sturdy workhorse of a camera. Its zoom lens gives excellent results. A professional camera for around £200.

• *ZINTEX XL* At £275 this is the cream of our selection. Fully automatic when required, shutter speed up to 1/4000 sec! Excellent viewfinder information for quick-decision photography. Standard 50mm lens, but zoom lens not too expensive at £65. Comes with sturdy carrying case.

ITEM 2: **Tutor's notes on photography assignment**

The aim of next term's main assignment is to explore the power, range and subtlety of photography as a medium of communication. A valuable approach to this is for you, in two groups of six students each, to photograph people, animals, objects and scenery in as wide a range of situations as possible, and then to select and display your pictures in a joint exhibition.

Buying your own equipment will be a big advantage, since much of your work will be done by groups or individuals outside normal working hours. But cameras and accessories are expensive and our £300 budget will have to be stretched, I'm afraid, to equip each group so that you can work simultaneously. Developing and printing costs can be met from existing funds – and we have free use of dark-room facilities for black-and-white processing.

ITEM 3: **Extract from *Get to Know your Camera,* a book on photography for beginners**

The 35 mm camera is easily the most popular camera because it is light to handle and versatile enough to cope with most forms of photography. There are two main types: the viewfinder (or 'compact') type, with a fixed lens in the less expensive ones; and the single lens reflex (SLR) type. The latter has the advantage of greater accuracy and flexibility, since subjects are viewed and focussed through the lens itself, and the camera can be fitted with different kinds of lenses to achieve very different effects – wide-angle for close-up shots and occasions when you want more in the picture without having to move back from the subject; and telephoto to enlarge distant objects and for portraits of people, animals, etc. Many photographers buy a zoom lens which allows variation between wide-angle and telephoto on one adjustable piece of equipment.

ITEM 4: **Your own notes**

Problem of cost. Do we split budget 50-50 between the groups & buy 2 identical sets of equipment? Or go for one expensive camera outfit plus one cheap/new or second-hand - then work out a rota for using them in turn? Or do we concentrate entirely on good-quality second-hand equipment (say 2 cameras per group)?

Group agrees that our priority for exhibition is variety of situations: really close-up shots of faces, animals, everyday objects; indoor studies using pubs, libraries, factories, buses, etc. (flashgun needed of course but we can get dramatic effects with natural light from a decent camera); high-speed action shots (need fast shutter speeds for these); atmospheric photos - sunsets, weather effects, light and shade; long-distance town & landscape studies, street life, the sea, etc.

Mustn't forget this is part of Communication course. Each photo has to speak for itself, so quality must be good - especially since we can get a lot of black-and-white pictures enlarged to poster size almost. Group agrees on essentials: sharp focus, frozen-action when it's needed, good use of lighting indoors or out, accurate framing... and some of us have hardly ever used a camera before!

ITEM 5: **Advertisement in local newspaper**

BENSONS FOR ALL YOUR PHOTOGRAPHIC NEEDS

Vast range of cameras and accessories of all kinds - NEW
and SECOND-HAND (all with guarantees).
Repairs carried out quickly and inexpensively.

Our friendly staff are only too happy to advise you, whether
you are a complete beginner or an advanced photographer.
Feel free to look round our extensive showroom.

J.W. BENSON LTD
Camera specialists
53 STATION PARADE NORTH
Tel. 57890

Questions

1   Carry out Planning Steps One to Seven.

2   Draft your introduction. Does it contain everything stated in the preface to this Guided Activity on pages 28–9?

3   Go on to draft the body of the report.

4   Work out your conclusion. In this case, it will take the form of a recommendation for the purchase of camera equipment in keeping with the nature of the assignment. Does your conclusion take account of all the relevant factors? Does it develop naturally out of the foregoing paragraphs?

FOCUS OF STUDY:
Objective and Subjective Reports

GUIDED ACTIVITY

In the report which follows, a controversial subject is presented. You are asked not to take sides over the issue, but to write impartially – that is, to adopt a neutral stance.

Report writing of this kind is *objective*. The writer takes up an impersonal stance in relation to the subject: his or her main purpose is to inform the reader about aspects which the writer has selected as being relevant. Although it is true to say that selecting and re-ordering are in themselves subjective decisions, the overall aim is nevertheless to present a clear, objective picture to the reader and not to convey an opinion or express personal feelings.

A subjective report, on the other hand, is one in which the focus is on the writer's opinion about the issue being dealt with. This opinion might be expressed directly, as in a recommendation or a decision, or it might be conveyed indirectly through the tone of the report: often there is a combination of direct and indirect means. In many cases the writer may choose to restrict the subjective element of the report to the last section, where, for example, a clear recommendation is to be made once possible courses of action or options have been outlined.

When reporting on subjects of a controversial nature, you must exercise great care in reading the instructions. If you are instructed to express an opinion, give advice, make a recommendation or decision, or justify a course of action, then clearly you are being asked to write a subjective report. If, however, your task is simply to inform your readers, or clarify an issue, or convey the views (often conflicting) of other people, then your report must be objective. Sometimes there is a fine line to be drawn between the two kinds of report; for example, you may be asked to report objectively on a dispute but to conclude by *suggesting* possible ways of resolving it. (See Activity Unit Seven for an example of this.) The report is still objective in this case because your suggestions are neither recommendations nor are they personal views: your aim here is to draw inferences from the dispute while maintaining a neutral stance.

Finally, there are reports which allow you to combine the two approaches. If, for instance, your task is to report on the year's activities of a club of which you are a member and then to highlight problems, successes, etc. for the consideration of other members reading your report, then your stance will be that of an interested party (subjective) who is providing information and drawing inferences from it for the consideration of other interested parties.

Plenty of practice in writing both subjective and objective reports – and combinations of these – will improve your skills not only in selecting, evaluating and organising the content of your reports but also in adapting the style of their language to the purposes they are meant to serve.

Study the following task, paying particular attention to the three stages of the instructions.

CROMBIE AIRPORT

The National Airports Authority (NAA) has put forward a proposal to keep Crombie Airport open for 24 hours a day incoming and departing flights. This proposal, supported by the Airport management, the local tourist organisations and travel agencies, has caused fierce controversy in and beyond the city of Crombie. The issue is to be the subject of a nationwide weekly radio programme dealing with controversial matters. You are a reporter for the programme and you have been asked to provide a report in the form of a radio script along the following lines:

a) a brief outline of the situation in the form of a fair and balanced account of the problem;

b) an examination of the conflicting interests which in your judgment underlie the dispute;

c) suggest, as a neutral observer, any possible ways in which the problem might be solved.

Write your report in approximately 350 words of formal continuous prose.

Your research into the problem has yielded the following items which should form the basis of your report.

ITEM 1: **Press statement by NAA (extract)**
... and it is therefore proposed that Crombie Airport be open for twenty-four hours a day with effect from 1st May next year. It is anticipated that, by extending its facilities to include night-time passenger arrivals and departures, the Airport will serve the people of Crombie and the surrounding region more effectively than at present. Mindful as we are of the concern about ground-level noise felt by residents close to flight paths, we nevertheless consider that the wider interests of the community are best served by the proposed expansion of business. We would, moreover, wish to reassure residents that all will be done to minimise aircraft noise during night flights, particularly during peak holiday periods. We would also remind the public that the Airport already handles mail and cargo flights during the night, and the proposed development should be seen as a natural extension of these activities.

ITEM 2: **Interview with Mr Howard McColl, Public Relations Officer, Crombie Airport**
This proposal is long overdue. If the people of this region are to have the genuine international airport that they are entitled to have, then we must introduce round-the-clock passenger

services as soon as possible. After all, nearly every other major conurbation in the U.K. enjoys such facilities, so why not Crombie? Look, the facts speak for themselves. Because of the ban on night passenger flights our air traffic business has been declining at a rate of five per cent each year for the last five years, while other airports have been handling increased business at a growth rate of up to twenty per cent because of the boom in holiday charter flights. We're losing passengers to the extent that we have actually had to cut back on airport staffing at a time of natural growth in the business! And we are talking about the jobs of Crombie people - make no mistake about that!

ITEM 3: Interview with Mrs Janet Ridgeworth, Secretary of Lister Vale Residents' Association

Q. You have recently started up a protest campaign. What are you protesting against?

A. We're against the whole idea of twenty-four hour flights over Lister Vale. The noise would be unbearable. We all accept that we are already under the airport's busiest flight paths and many of us bought houses here knowing that we have to put up with a certain amount of aircraft noise. But we had been assured by the airport people that jets would getting quieter (I must admit some of them are) and we would at least be undisturbed at night. We certainly didn't expect a proposal like this!

Q. But what about assurances from the NAA about reduced ground-level noise now that most planes climb faster straight after take-off?

A. Yes, take-offs are often quieter than they used to be. But they've done nothing about the approach runs into the airport. The noise can be ear-splitting and you never get used to it the way you do road traffic or trains.

Q. Surely, though, the benefits to Crombie as a whole outweigh such considerations?

A. I thought that in any democracy the voices of minority groups had a right to be heard! In any case, there are quite enough daytime flights from Crombie to other British airports for holidaymakers to catch planes to all the exotic places they want to visit. Or they can travel by coach to any of these airports - there are excellent link services now. Why can't Crombie Airport work at improving these options?

ITEM 4: Comments from passengers and officials in the departure lounge at Crombie Airport

a) Night flights for passengers? I'm all for it. At the end of our holiday last summer our return flight from Malta to Crombie was delayed by an hour. This meant we would fail to beat the midnight deadline at Crombie, so we had to divert to Halchester Airport. What a way to end a holiday - no coaches laid on so there was nothing for it but to make a 60 mile taxi journey back to Crombie at 1.30 in the morning!

b) I've been a clerk in the baggage section here for fifteen years and this is the best news I've had for a long time. We should be getting thousands more passengers coming through, and that means job security for all of us. And new jobs, too, once the system really starts ticking over. O.K., so a few people in posh houses are complaining they'll be losing some of their beauty sleep next summer. Try telling that to the unemployed folk round here.

c) I'm waiting for the next shuttle flight so that I can catch the 747 to New York. To be honest I don't find it a problem not being able to fly direct from here. Lots of people like me enjoy flying for its own sake and I reckon you should allow plenty of time anyway for your total journey. Service in this airport is good. Round-the-clock flights might allow them to introduce new routes and bigger airlines but won't it spoil the character of this place - small and friendly?

ITEM 5: Interview with local travel agent

Well, on the whole we welcome the proposal, though I don't think the local coach and bus operators will once they begin to lose the revenue from 20,000 or so holidaymakers each year who have to catch their flights from Halchester and other airports. For us it means we can book a lot of extra package tours direct from Crombie and that means a wider choice of resorts for people here. But what about visitors staying at the new hotel and conference complex near the airport? Are they going to be so keen to come here after next summer?

ITEM 6: Readings from your decibel counter

Recording made on 10 July at home of Mrs Ridgeworth, during the late morning period:

1) Noise from passing traffic on nearby main road: between 70 and 90 decibels.

2) Noise from 737 plane taking off and climbing away: a peak level of 105 decibels.

3) Noise from several planes (different types) making approach runs into the airport: betweem 70 and 100 decibels.

Questions

1 Having analysed the 'report situation' and completed your checklist and overview, what problems do you think you will have in carrying out the instructions under (a), (b) and (c)? Consider especially the terms 'fair and balanced account', 'conflicting interests' and 'as a natural observer'.

2   In carrying out Steps Four and Five make sure you get a clear idea of the two sides of the controversy in order to comply with instructions (a) and (b).

3   Staying with Steps Four and Five, which points do you find relevant to instruction (c)? Can you suggest any points which in your judgment might be developed as a possible solution to the problem?

4   Now draft out your report, providing a suitable introduction. Make sure your conclusion, like the rest of the report, is appropriate to the objective nature of the task. Pay particular attention to your expression: avoid, for example, saying things like 'I think' or 'in my opinion' and use impersonal expressions such as 'it may be considered that' or 'it may appear that'.

5   It might be helpful at this point to refer to the advice on 'Style' in Section Three of this book. Check through your first draft and alter anything which you think is weak or inconsistent in the style of your writing.

6   Compare your first draft with other people's work.

7   Now write your final version of this report.

FURTHER PRACTICE

1   Choose a topic on which you know there are conflicting views. Research your subject by gathering evidence for these conflicting views and assemble your information in whatever form will be helpful to the writing of an objective report. Decide on your terms of reference and then write the report.

2   Using the same data, or gathering data on a fresh topic, write a subjective report, or a report that combines an objective stance with the expression of a considered opinion at the end. Again, make your terms of reference clear.

Suggested topics for this work:
Law and order / Crime and punishment
Energy production and conservation (including the 'nuclear debate')
Bloodsports
Animal experimentation
Equality of the sexes
Censorship of the press, cinema and television
Dealing with terrorism
Freedom of speech
Environmental pollution
Rights of smokers and non-smokers
'Progress' versus 'Conservation' and 'Heritage'
Competitive sport (for example, the question of amateurism and professionalism)

FOCUS OF STUDY:
Complete report exercises for further practice

INTRODUCTION

Through working on Units One to Six you have learned to analyse, plan and complete a range of reporting tasks. It now remains for you to practise your report-writing skills without the help of Guided Activities.

Before you tackle the following exercises, re-read the step-by-step guide in the first section of this book (pages 6–14) to make sure you cover all the main points. Bear in mind that, by now, the planning steps should be more or less automatic to your thinking with the result that your total time for writing a report should be less than it used to be.

If you experience any difficulties, try to identify your problem and go back to the relevant Activity Unit in order to help yourself to solve it.

Exercises

(1) CUSTOMERS' COMPLAINTS

You have recently been appointed to the managerial staff of Arrow Supermarkets. You are responsible for customer relations in three stores in your area. One of your first tasks has been to examine customers' complaints over the past twelve months and to report to the area manager with recommendations for improvements.

Your research has produced various items of material, detailed below. Incorporating relevant points from these, write your report in an appropriate style in approximately 400 words. Your report, suitably introduced and concluded, should be planned thus:

a)   customers' complaints viewed in the general context of store-customer relations;
b)   pattern of complaints in the three stores over the year period;
c)   brief indication of the more serious trends;
d)   brief statement of your recommendations at this stage.

ITEM 1: Memo from your predecessor (relevant extract)

... In my experience, customers make their
dissatisfaction known in the following ways: by
letter to the management (relatively infrequently),
by telephone, by personal complaint to the
information desk (sometimes after direct
communication with check-out staff). Letters are
automatically passed on to Customer Relations for
reply. I have always tried to respond to the
customer as quickly as possible, remedying the
problem where appropriate, but sometimes replies
are delayed through pressure of work - any ideas
for improvement here? Telephone calls are usually
switched to this office: if I'm not available I try
to get back to the customer within the day. All
complaints made in person to our store staff are
noted by the information desk personnel. Routine
matters, whether or not remedied by store
management, are brought to our attention in the
form of written daily memos sent to this office. If
store management cannot resolve these spoken
complaints then I am usually summoned to the store
to deal with them face-to-face with the customer.
Bearing in mind our furthest store is twelve miles
from this office, this can prove time-consuming and
not always the most efficient way of dealing with
the problem.

Most complaints are genuine and many are conveyed
courteously, even apologetically, by the customer. These
are generally straightforward situations to deal with,
particularly those concerned with spoilt, damaged or faulty
goods. My formula here is: apologise; replace or refund;
and (if appropriate) offer a compensatory gift in addition.
But apart from the problem of deciding in some cases
whether the complaint is genuine, and what to do if it is
not, you will have the more complex complaints to deal with
- particularly those against store personnel for alleged
discourtesy, poor service, and so on. Senior management
tell us that the customer is always right, but applying
this principle while at the same time reassuring staff of
fairness in our investigations constitutes our biggest
headache.

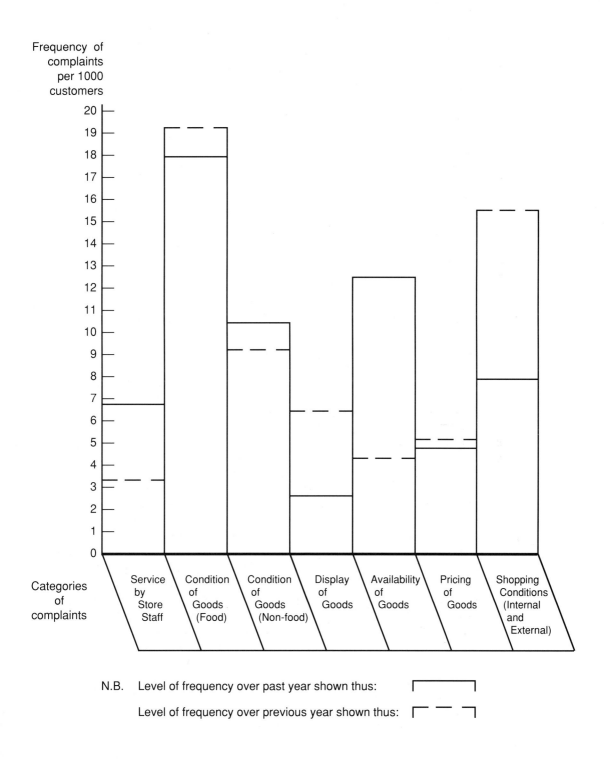

ITEM 2: **Bar Chart showing comparative frequencies of customers complaints over past two years in three branches of Arrow Supermarkets.**

Frequency of complaints per 1000 customers

Categories of complaints

| Service by Store Staff | Condition of Goods (Food) | Condition of Goods (Non-food) | Display of Goods | Availability of Goods | Pricing of Goods | Shopping Conditions (Internal and External) |

N.B. Level of frequency over past year shown thus:

Level of frequency over previous year shown thus:

Manager of Store A

Since the car-park extension was completed ten months ago, we've not only increased our sales volume but our shoppers seem more relaxed somehow. Maybe it's because they've no longer the hassle of getting parked at a meter and having to watch their time. Now there's space for everyone and more time to shop! ... Fresh produce is the biggest source of complaint, followed by bread and cakes. I suspect most people who return these keep them too long in their kitchen cupboards and still expect them to stay fresh. But if there's proof of reasonably recent purchase we don't quibble... We're getting a few more complaints against check-out staff these days but I suppose that's inevitable now that our trading is busier.

Manager of Store B

The trouble with Joe Public is that he's never satisfied no matter what you do. Last year we decided to discontinue three of our slower-selling ranges - do-it-yourself, garden-care and kitchenware - and we utilised the space by renting it out to a double-glazing firm. The sales rep. has an eye-catching stand and hands out leaflets to our shoppers. Nice little money-maker, that, but now we're getting criticised for no longer stocking things that people didn't seem to want anyway! Check-out assistants? My deputy reckons we need to improve our training programme - he's a bit edgy about some of the complaints we're getting about their attitude - but I don't see how we can find the time.

Manager of Store C

Last year we reorganised the dairy produce and frozen food areas, and then we improved the lighting and display signs right through the store. Shoppers can find what they want faster now - we don't get so many exasperated queries about where things are kept... Another positive trend is greater customer satisfaction (or at least fewer complaints!) with our check-out system. Customers' cheques now have to be validated at the information desk by specially trained staff (we cash cheques there as well), so shoppers are no longer held up in long queues waiting for assistants to send for supervisors to process cheques and credit cards. Of course, our new point-of-sale computer system is also speeding up customers' payments... We've taken on more school-leavers and other trainees to deal specifically with the 'cosmetics' side of things: tidying and restocking shelves, retrieving trolleys, keeping the floor clean, maintaining safe conditions, and the like. Unlike my predecessor here, I don't regard these as menial jobs; they're an essential part of staff training. Some of these young people are potential managers... I've also plans to start up a fortnightly 'ideas' session as part of our staff training programme in which <u>anyone</u> from myself to our latest recruit can offer suggestions for improving things... I'd appreciate your help with one thing. I'm worried about our competitors beating Arrow in the health food stakes. We've been turning away too many customers who come in looking for wholefood products, vegetarian items, or whatever. We're not getting any guidance from HQ about food and non-food items using animal-free products or free from animal-testing. There's an increasing demand for these and we're not meeting it. I've letters to prove it.

(2) CRIME PREVENTION

This task requires a somewhat longer piece of writing than previous ones. You are asked to write a 500-word report on ways in which members of the public can co-operate with the police to prevent crime, basing your material on the items which follow. In this task you are not required to adopt a specific role as a writer, but your stance should be consistently objective and you should employ a suitably formal style appropriate to the purpose of informing a wide readership. The main stages of the report are for you to work out, and there should be an effective introduction and conclusion.

ITEM 1: **Extract from Home Office publication,** *Practical ways to Crack Crime.*
Extract A

CRIME: REVERSING THE TREND

Crime, as we are all aware, has been a growing problem all over the world in the last 30 years. But we are not powerless against crime. Much is being done – and more can be done – to reverse the trend. You can play a part in it.

The first step towards preventing crime is understanding its nature. Most crime is against property, not people. And most is not carried out by professionals; nor is it carefully planned. Property crimes thrive on the easy opportunity. They are often committed by adolescents and young men, the majority of whom stop offending as they grow older – the peak age for offending is 15.

This reliance by criminals on the easy opportunity is the key to much crime prevention. Motor cars, for example, are a sitting target for the criminal. The police estimate that 70–90% of car crime results from easy opportunities. Surveys have shown that approximately one in five drivers do not always bother to secure their cars by locking all the doors and shutting all the windows.

It's the same story with our homes. In approximately 30% of domestic burglaries the burglar simply walks in without needing to use force; the householder has left a door unlocked or window open.

If opportunities like these did not exist, criminals would have a much harder time. The chances are that many crimes would not be committed at all, which would in turn release more police time for tackling serious crime.

Of course, the primary responsibility for coping with crime rests with the police and the courts. But there are ways that you can help reverse the trend.

Extract B

PROTECT YOUR HOME AND PROPERTY

More than 900,000 burglaries take place in Britain each year.

That is one out of every 25 homes. Go round your own home and take a look. Do all the windows have locks? Do you have good security locks on your doors? Or are you making things easy for thieves?

Until you're burgled, it's difficult to imagine just how unpleasant it is. Your personal things are rifled, your most valuable possessions are stolen, your peace of mind is shattered. But it doesn't have to happen.

Taking simple precautions works. Here's why:

Most burglars are not highly skilled professionals
They're looking for easy pickings...an empty home, an unlocked window, a door without a proper deadlock. Thieves can be stopped.

They don't like locked windows
Breaking glass makes noise and attracts attention. If the window is properly locked, they won't be able to open it even after breaking the glass. Which means that, to get in, they would have to climb past jagged edges of broken glass.

They don't like doors with security deadlocks
It's more difficult to get in. These locks can't be opened without a key. That means the burglar can't just break a pane of glass in the door, reach in, and undo the latch.

The effect of sensible precautions adds up
Using good locks on all doors and windows, marking your property,

joining a Neighbourhood Watch Scheme...all these things work. And they work best when they work together.

Of course, no one is saying you can make your home 100% burglar-proof. But it's a fact that thieves try to reduce their risks by going for easy targets. So you can make your home so difficult to get into that they'll go elsewhere. And that's got to be worthwhile. It needn't cost a fortune either. £50 spent on the average home will make it much more secure. Even a few pounds spent wisely is money well spent.

The only question left is how to go about doing it. That's what this leaflet is all about.

Ask your local police
If you'd like more information, however, see your local Crime Prevention Officer. You can call him at your local police station. He'll be happy to visit your home and give you free advice.

Extract C

Crooks come in many disguises. These are just a few of them...

The bogus 'official'. Seemingly respectable and smartly dressed, he may claim to be from the council, the water board or some other organisation. He may even claim to be a solicitor. But his real purpose is to trick his way into your home to see what he can steal.

The bogus 'dealer' may offer to buy your furniture or other items at what may seem to be a good price. But the chances are that he is trying to trick you into parting with something at well below its true value.

If you want to sell something try to get it properly valued by a genuine dealer or ask a friend or relative for their advice.

The bogus 'workmen'. They say that they need to come in to check something, or make urgent repairs. Again, they really want to come in to steal.

When someone calls this is what to do...

- Before you open the door put the chain on. (If you haven't got one it's a good idea to have one fitted. They don't cost much.) If you have a door viewer, check to see who it is.

- If you don't know them, ask to see their identity card. Be sure to check it carefully. Genuine callers won't mind.

- If you are unsure, ask the caller to return later. In the meantime you can check their story by phoning the organisation or company they claim to represent. Don't let them pressure you.

- If you are suspicious, phone your local police and tell them what has happened. Better safe than sorry.

Remember, bogus callers can be men, women or even children. They may work on their own, or there could be two or more. Their stories may seem plausible, but they're out to steal - from you!

PRACTICAL WAYS TO PREVENT CRIME

Your family

Violent crimes are still comparatively rare: they account for only a very small part of all recorded crime. Statistically, therefore, the chance that you or a member of your family will be a victim is already low. Nevertheless, many people are frightened that they, or someone close to them, will be the victim of physical assault, mugging or rape. The risk of this happening can be reduced still further by taking sensible precautions.

How Women Can Protect themselves

If you are a man, don't stop reading.

Although this information is mainly for women, you should be aware of it too.

The best way to minimise the risk of an attack is by taking these precautions:

When at Home

Check and, if necessary, strengthen, the security of your house or flat.

Draw your curtains after dark to discourage any Peeping Tom. If you think there is a prowler outside, don't go out to check – dial 999.

Use only your surname and initials in the telephone directory and on the doorplate if you live in a flat. That way, a stranger cannot tell whether a man or woman lives there.

If you get home and notice sign of a break-in – a broken window, say, or the door ajar – do not go in or call out: the intruder could still be inside. Go to a neighbour's house to call the police.

When you are at home keep external doors locked. A telephone extension installed in the bedroom would also be worthwhile.

When moving into a new home it makes sense to change the front and back door locks – other people may still have keys that fit. *Never* forget to use the locks!

If you are selling your home, try not to show people around on your own. Ask your estate agent to send a representative with prospective buyers.

When answering the telephone don't give your number. If the caller claims to have a wrong number ask him or her to repeat the number required. Never reveal any information about yourself to a stranger and never say you are alone in the house.

If you receive abusive or obscene telephone calls put the receiver down immediately. Don't say anything – an emotional reaction is what the caller wants. If the calls continue, tell the police and keep a record of the date, time and content of each call as this may help the authorities to trace the caller.

Out on foot

Avoid short-cuts through dimly lit alleys or across waste ground.

Walk facing the traffic so a car cannot pull up behind you unnoticed. Walk on the street side of the pavement, so an attacker lurking in an alley has further to come to reach you.

If a car does approach you and you are threatened, scream and run away in the opposite direction – this will gain you vital seconds and make it more difficult for the car driver to follow. If you can, make a note of the number and description of the car.

Don't hitch-hike or accept lifts from strangers.

Cover up expensive looking jewellery.

If you are going to be out late, try to arrange a lift home or book a taxi. When you get home, ask the driver to wait until you are inside.

If you regularly walk home after dark, consider buying a screech alarm, available from the security sections of many DIY shops. Their piercing noise can frighten off an attacker. Carry the alarm in your hand, not in a bag where it may be difficult to reach in an emergency.

If you are carrying a handbag, keep it close to your body. Keep your house keys in a separate pocket. If someone does grab the bag, let it go rather than risk injury by fighting. Your safety is more important than your property.

If you think someone is following you on foot, cross the street – more than once if necessary – to check your suspicions. If you are still suspicious, run to the nearest place where there will be other people – a pub, launderette or any house with plenty of lights on. Call the police as soon as you get to a safe place. But don't call from a phonebox in the street: the attacker could trap you inside.

If you regularly go jogging or cycling, try to vary your route and time so you can't be waylaid by an attacker. Stick to well-lit roads with pavements.

Self-defence classes can help you to deal with an attack and give you a feeling of greater confidence. Ask your local police if they run classes. Some employers also run classes for female employees. If yours does not, you may like to suggest it.

On public transport

Particularly after dark try to avoid using isolated bus stops. On a bus, sit near the driver or conductor.

On a train, sit in a compartment where there are several other people – ideally in a compartment which will be near the exit at your destination.

When driving

Before going on any long journey make sure your vehicle is in good condition. Plan your route in advance, using main roads as far as possible, and have enough money and petrol. It's also worth carrying a spare petrol can. If you can, telephone before leaving to give your estimated time of arrival and route. Carry some change or a phonecard to make a public telephone call if you need to.

Be wary of hitch-hikers. If somebody flags you down on a quiet road, make sure it is a genuine emergency before you open a window or get out of the car. If you are in any doubt go on and call the police.

Keep your doors locked when driving in town and valuables away from open windows.

After dark, always park in a well-lit, preferably busy area – and take a moment or two to look around before you get out.

When you come back to your car have your key ready and check there is no one in the car.

If you are having problems try to get as near to a telephone as possible. On a motorway look for the marker arrows and follow them – they show the direction of the nearest 'phone. While on the hard shoulder, or telephoning, keep a sharp look out and do not accept lifts from strangers; wait for the police or breakdown service.

If the worst happens

It is sensible to think about what you would be prepared to do if you were physically attacked. Could you fight back or would you play along and wait for a chance to escape? Preparing yourself for all possibilities could provide a split-second advantage.

If you are cornered or threatened, and there are people nearby who can help, shout and scream to try to attract their attention.

If you are actually attacked only *you* can decide whether to fight back. A woman who is being attacked has every right to defend herself with reasonable force. An umbrella, hairspray or your car keys are all examples of items often carried and which can be used against an attacker.

What the law does *not* allow is carrying anything which can be described as an offensive weapon. This includes any items which have been specially adapted, such as a sharpened comb, or a knife carried in self-defence.

ITEM 2: Neighbourhood Watch (Home Office Publication)

Essentially a way to improve the sense of safety, security and local community in the area, *Neighbourhood Watches* are now a well-established part of crime prevention.

The first *Neighbourhood Watch* scheme was established in 1982: now there are almost 60 000 watch schemes throughout the country covering an estimated 3.5 million households – more than one household in every six. In rural villages they might include just a few households, whereas large urban schemes can cover up to 5000 homes. They also have many names – *Neighbourhood Watch, Home Watch, Community Watch, Tower Watch* – but all are based on the same idea.

Why set up a Neighbourhood Watch scheme?

Schemes usually start because residents or the police in an area identify a crime problem and want to reduce it. However, the benefits of setting up a watch can go beyond reducing the level of crime in the scheme area. It can also reduce the fear of crime in a neighbourhood, and encourage good relations between the police and the community. It can also help residents get to know one another.

How does Neighbourhood Watch work?

There are three basic ways in which all members of a scheme can help the police reduce crime and fear of crime in their area:

(a) Looking out for your neighbourhood. Residents of watch areas are encouraged to be on the look-out for suspicious behaviour. All police forces are ready to offer guidance on what to look out for and the information they need when you report anything; watch schemes are not intended to encourage members of the public to 'have a go' or set themselves up as a vigilante force apart from the police. Watch has always been, and must remain, a partnership between the police and the public: the public are the eyes and ears, but the police retain their active role when dealing with actual or suspected crime.

(b) Securing the home. To reduce the attractiveness of their home to the opportunist thief, householders are given advice on how to improve their security. They are also encouraged to use security already installed and to look after the homes of other scheme members when they are away.

(c) Property marking. Schemes might also include householders marking their property with post-coding equipment. This is often owned by the scheme, paid for by fund-raising or business sponsorship. Or it might be donated by, for example, a local crime prevention panel.

ITEM 3: **Comments from people affected by crimes**

PERSON A: My husband and I were devastated when we came back from the cinema to find our house had been broken into. As it happens, whoever did it didn't steal very much, and apart from some money what was taken we'd had insured. But that's not the point. It's the feeling of being violated, you know, some evil-minded stranger invading your privacy ... And what a mess! We've redecorated the whole place since then but I still get nightmares. The police advised us about trying to make the house as near to burglar-proof as possible because there could always be a next time.

PERSON B: I've worked on the railways for thirty years nearly and I can honestly say I've never known such vandalism as there's been over the last three years. Not just on the trains and in stations, either - there's stones thrown at the

windows of moving trains and heavy objects
deliberately left near the lines. One day
there'll be a derailment if we don't do something
to stop this. The public could be more aware of
what's happening - anything suspicious could be
reported - and we might be able to help the
police to catch these vandals. After all it's
everyone's railway, not just ours.

PERSON C: Being mugged was always something that happened
to other people - never me! Then when it did
happen I kept asking, 'Why me?' You hear about
'victims of crime' and that's just what people
like me are: victims. There were just two of them
who jumped me in a surprise attack. Who'd've
thought it? There were actually houses nearby
with lights on and a couple of cars drove past -
it wasn't late, so surely someone should've
noticed. They got my wallet and brief-case, of
course. It was pure timing. I tried to fight them
off but they had the advantage. I heard that more
of us blokes get mugged than women do but I
reckon that's because hardly any women dare go
out alone after dark anyway. Why can't we all get
together and do something about this?

SECTION THREE

The Language of Reports

Many people consider the hardest part of writing to be finding the exact words to express their thoughts rather than arriving at the thoughts themselves. They assume that the content of what we write and the 'words-to-express' this content are separate matters – as if the former were the body and the latter the clothes. On the contrary, thought and language are much more closely connected than is often realised. Thinking out *what* we want to write and deciding *how* we want to write it are really two sides of the same coin.

We are all aware how fluently we can talk when we relax in casual conversation: we say things just as they come into our minds and we reply spontaneously to what other people say. On formal occasions, however, such as interviews for jobs, we are more conscious of what we should say and how we should say it, and we find ourselves 'rehearsing' our comments and replies to make sure they are right before committing ourselves to them. The 'rehearsal' may take only a moment but it still makes the difference between spontaneity and deliberate planning. And we plan *in* language by first expressing to ourselves what we intend to express to others.

Like speech, writing involves interpersonal behaviour, with different ways of responding to informal and formal situations. As a report writer meeting other people's requirements you should recognise the formality of the task and rehearse what needs to be written and how it needs to be written. Like the interviewee you will be guided by your sense of purpose and sense of 'audience' (readership).

In report writing, then, the final version needs to use forms of language appropriate to a formal situation. The characteristics of this kind of language are now described.

PART 1
STYLE, EXPRESSION AND GRAMMAR

Style in language can range from the casual and colloquial to the very formal. In other words, language is used in different ways according to the situation. The term 'situation' in this sense comprises the following features:

(1) the **context** of the communication – the circumstances in which language is being used (e.g. in a coffee-shop, in a classroom, at an auction, at a wedding);

(2) the **subject** that is being talked or written about;

(3) the **relationship** between the speaker/writer and listener/reader;

(4) the **purpose** of the communication.

You will notice that the last three of these features correspond to the things we ask ourselves when we plan a report (see the planning checklist in Section One). This is because the selection and ordering of material for a report are governed by the situation – and so is our style of writing.

There is no single 'correct' style of speaking or writing. A doctor discussing a patient's symptoms with a colleague will adopt a different style from the one normally used for talking to the patient: a holiday-maker writing a letter of complaint to a tour operator will convey the same message in a different style in a letter to a relative. As language users we learn through experience to formulate widely differing styles that are *appropriate* to given situations.

In most situations that require a written report, it is a formal style that is appropriate. Even here there is room for variation since writer–reader relationships range in report writing across a spectrum. A report on an industrial accident may require the extreme formality of a legal document, while the kind of report dealt with in Activity Unit Five (choosing cameras) can be written in a relaxed style without losing its formality.

In Activity Unit Four we considered an important aspect of style – the use of **tone** in writing. Tone reveals the writer's attitude to the subject and reader. We said that a consistently formal and neutral tone is generally considered to be appropriate to report writing; the aim is to establish the right relationship between writer and reader and at the same time convey the writer's purpose clearly. In addition, there are two other factors that help us to characterise style as 'formal' or 'informal': **expression** and **grammatical** choice.

Expression is concerned with the meanings of words and word-groups. Written expression succeeds when it conveys the writer's message effectively to the reader, that is, when it conveys what the writer wants to say to an intended reader or group of readers with the minimum risk of misunderstanding. In informal situations, such as casual conversation among friends or personal letters, the exact form of one's spoken or written expression is not as crucial as in formal situations because other kinds of communication (for example, gestures) help to get meaning across or repetition and other forms of verbal reinforcement are acceptable ('What I mean to say is ...', 'Oh, I forgot to mention...' and so on). But in a report, expression stands on its own: the words on the page must speak for themselves fluently, clearly and economically.

What, then, makes for effective expression in formal writing? It is probably easier to point out some of the faults that make it ineffective so that they can be avoided in report writing.

The first is *unintentional ambiguity*. An expression is ambiguous when meanings other than the one intended by the writer may be inferred by the reader. Consider the following examples.

'McClelland raced towards the goal and instead of passing shot himself.'

The unwanted implication of a footballer's suicide is caused by a common type of ambiguity known as ellipsis, leaving out words needed to complete a statement. (Ellipsis in itself is not a fault: it becomes one when its use causes misunderstanding.)

'Having arrived late for the third time in succession, the manager dismissed the trainee clerk.'

'Reaching sixty-five, a gold watch was given to him as a retirement gift.'

In each case here a participial phrase is misrelated to the person or thing it should describe and the sentence should be restructured.

'The doctors in this practice only visit patients at home if they phone the surgery before 9.00 am'

The misplaced 'only' implies that visiting patients at home is all they do. Common-sense tells us that 'they' refers to the patients, not the doctors, but in other contexts unidentified pronouns can lead to ambiguity. And is 'before 9.00 am' on the same day as the requested visit or the day before?

'We are visiting a factory in an industrial park which is being expanded.'

The adjectival clause ('which...expanded') is too far removed from its antecedent 'factory' if the writer intends expansion to apply to the building rather than the whole park.

A second fault in expression that often occurs in formal writing is *verbosity*, the use of too many words to say something. At the opposite extreme from ellipsis, verbosity frequently occurs when a writer wishes to impress instead of opting for straightforward expression; or sometimes the use of a lot of words acts as camouflage to hide imprecise thinking. How do you react to the following notice?

'No animals of the canine variety, under any circumstances other than those pertaining to the purpose of acting in the role of guides, may be granted permission to gain admittance to any part, section or area of these premises.'

It would be simpler to write: 'No dogs, other than guide-dogs, are allowed to enter these premises'. Of course, few writers are as long-winded as this, but most of us are guilty of verbosity to some degree. Your aim should be to cultivate economy of expression, saying enough to get your message across without choking it with verbal overkill.

Confused or *misused* words are another source of weakness in expression. You should take care to distinguish clearly between each word in the following pairs:

accept/except	lay/lie
affect/effect	license/licence
allusion/illusion	loose/lose

altogether/all together	luxuriant/luxurious
complement/compliment	moral/morale
continual/continuous	passed/past
councillor/counsellor	personal/personnel
dependant/dependent	practicable/practical
disinterested/uninterested	practice/practise
disorganised/unorganised	precede/proceed
emigrate/immigrate	principal/principle
everyday/every day	respectfully/respectively
exhaustive/exhausted	successfully/successively
imply/infer	there/their
its/it's	who's/whose

Closely related to expression is another aspect of style – *grammatical choice*. It goes without saying that 'good grammar' is essential to formal writing (we saw examples of grammatical faults just now when we looked at ambiguity of expression): what we are concerned with here is not grammatical errors but stylistic choice – the choice between alternative correct grammatical forms. Two kinds of grammatical choice are particularly relevant to report writing: reported (indirect) speech or direct speech, and the active voice or the passive voice.

Reported speech is a grammatical form allowing us to convey the gist of what someone has said more economically than by quoting the whole speech. Saving words is not the only purpose, since this technique also imparts a more impersonal tone to a report, particularly if strongly worded opinions are expressed by the speaker. Here is a report in direct speech:

> The foreman said, 'If you want my opinion, the whole works should be inspected and pretty fast too. The treatment plant has already gone haywire three times this year – last month it would have blown sky-high if we hadn't got to the effluent valves in time. The men are in complete agreement with me, by the way, but does anyone listen to us? No way. We're thinking of some kind of action to *make* them listen but our hands are tied, aren't they? Anyway, the whole work-force are getting together next week to sort out what will have to be done about safety round here.'

Here is a version in reported speech:

> The foreman claimed full support from his men in demanding urgent inspection of the whole works. The treatment plant had already malfunctioned three times during the year and would have exploded the previous month but for prompt attention to the effluent valves. The foreman admitted limited scope for action in bringing attention to the problem but a meeting on safety would be held by the whole work-force the following week.

It could also be summarised more briefly:

> The foreman announced that a meeting of the whole work-force would be held the following week to discuss what would have to be done about safety.

He was urging a full works inspection following a series of malfunctions in the treatment plant during the year.

The grammatical rules for conversion from direct to reported speech are concerned with *pronouns* ('I' to 'he', for example); *tenses* (each tense goes one step into the past –'has malfunctioned' to 'had malfunctioned', 'will have to be done' to 'would have to be done', though 'would have' remains the same) and *expressions of time* such as 'last month' (becomes 'the previous month'). You will notice in the illustrated conversion some changes in expression and tone to produce an effect that is more in keeping with the formal style of a report.

Our second kind of grammatical choice is between *active voice* and *passive voice* when we are reporting actions. If, for example, we know the plumber turned off the water supply we can say, 'The plumber has turned off the water supply' (active voice) or 'The water supply has been turned off by the plumber' (passive voice, 'plumber' the agent of the action). If we do not know who is responsible, we can use the passive voice without an agent: 'The water supply has been turned off'. This last version is preferable in formal styles of speaking or writing to the informal 'Someone has turned off the water supply'. The passive voice is not intrinsically 'better' or 'more correct' than the active voice. It is simply an appropriate form to use in reports.

Our first reason, then, for choosing the passive voice in formal reports is to express an action when the agent is unknown or only vaguely known. In casual conversation we might say, 'They've gone and ruined the town centre with those hideous new shops' (architects? town planners? the shop-keepers?) and it sounds natural. A formal version would be: 'The town centre has been ruined by those ...'. In addition, we can use the passive form of a verb when we are more interested in what has happened to someone or something rather than who was responsible for the action. For example, 'The conductor collapsed and was taken to hospital' may be more appropriate than 'The conductor collapsed and an ambulance took him to hospital'. The passive voice is useful to the report writer in another way: it can help to sustain a formal style by making a statement more impersonal than if expressed in active form, as in the following illustration: 'It is not yet known how many sheep have been lost in the blizzards, but it is feared that the figure might well be above three hundred' rather than 'We do not know yet ... but people fear that ...'. Finally, we can use the passive to maintain stylistic fluency as a way of avoiding having to make an awkward change of subject within a sentence: 'The pathologist appeared in court this morning and was asked some very searching questions by the counsel for the defence' has a more fluent style than'The pathologist appeared in court this morning and the counsel for the defence asked him some very searching questions'.

Style, then, is largely a matter of choosing varieties of tone, expression and grammar that suit the situation. As writers and speakers we have a repertoire of stylistic features. The more we practise a particular form of communication, in our case written reports, the more skilful we become in making the most effective choices for different purposes and audiences.

PART 2
STRUCTURE

In the Activity Units in Section Two there are suggested outlines to help you construct your reports paragraph by paragraph. This kind of guidance is not always given in report writing tasks, and even if it is there are still some skills which you should learn if you want your reports to hold together well. These skills are grouped under the term 'structure'.

Structure in writing is the ordering and linking of parts to make up a unified whole, be it a novel, a business letter or a newspaper article. You are familiar with the organisation of words, phrases and clauses into full sentences. What we are also concerned with here is the overall structure of a report made up of complete sentences and paragraphs. Effective overall structure requires skill in handling three of the writer's 'building tools': exposition, cohesion and linkage.

A good report should contain, in its introductory paragraph, a clear *exposition* of the theme of the report . 'Exposition' is the noun form of 'expound', which means to lay out in detail, to interpret clearly for the benefit of someone else. The purpose of your report should also be clearly identified (theme and purpose are closely linked) and, if necessary in your judgment, something of the nature of the relationship with your reader or readers. The introductory paragraph should contain in miniature the material to be developed in the rest of the report.

Subsequent paragraphs should then fulfil the expectations set up in the reader's mind by the introduction. Short stories and 'whodunit' novels may keep the reader in suspense and have twists in their tails but not reports. Even if your report is to include a decision or recommendation in its conclusion, the development of your exposition throughout the paragraphs should offer the reader a smooth, logical transition from start to finish. The final section should not come as a surprise.

Cohesion refers to the property of a text where all the parts are logically related to form a unified whole. In a cohesive piece of writing the arrangement and linking of ideas makes the message clearer. If there is poor cohesion the report comes across as a collection of loosely related statements and the message is confused.

What are the features of a cohesive report? In the first place the tone will be consistent throughout, as indeed will other aspects of the writer's style. Secondly, there will be a unity of ideas within each paragraph, that is, the ideas should all relate to the one topic of the paragraph. It is common to start a paragraph with a 'topic sentence' both as a marker for a new stage in the development of the exposition and as a statement of what the rest of the paragraph deals with. Structurally, sentences may (and should) vary within a paragraph but thematically they should not. Thirdly, there should be a sense of purpose being fulfilled by the time the reader reaches the final paragraph. This may be achieved by means of a brief summary or review of main points; on the other hand, this may not be considered necessary (particularly if it is a short report) as long as the concluding paragraph satisfies the reader that what was raised in the first paragraph has been settled in the last.

A fourth feature of cohesion is worth considering in more detail since it is a 'building tool' in its own right. *Linkage*, the use of connective words and phrases, provides a system of verbal signposts that reinforce the logical relationships in the piece of writing. These linking devices are indispensable allies of the writer in composing a well-structured report. They may be classified as follows.

a) The words *'this'*, *'these'*, *'that'*, and *'those'* either as demonstrative adjectives (as in 'these problems') or as pronouns standing for nouns. These humble little words are really quite powerful because by referring back to topics in previous sentences or paragraphs they signal links with others being introduced.

b) *Synonyms*. As different ways of saying the same thing, synonyms can help to avoid monotony of expression while linking different aspects of the same topic. To illustrate this, the topic-word 'complaint' might be linked to a new point by synonyms such as 'grievance', 'criticism', 'charge', 'imputation', 'expression of discontent/disquiet/dissatisfaction'. Care should be taken to retain the same tone by avoiding slang or colloquial terms, such as 'moan', 'gripe' or 'chip on the shoulder'!

c) *Generalisations*. Used in a similar way to synonyms, generalisations are valuable linking words while at the same time contributing to economy of expression. The phrase, 'these issues', might refer back to a group of points dealt with in a previous paragraph; or the word 'generosity' might sum up a group of common attitudes to be examined.

d) *Connectives*. A variety of logical relationships can be signalled by the following words and phrases – because, since, as, for this reason, (**reason**); so, therefore, hence, as a result, consequently, accordingly, thus (**result**); although, but, however, nevertheless, notwithstanding (**qualification**); furthermore, moreover, in addition, indeed, in fact (**addition** or **amplification**); on the one hand ... on the other hand, whereas, instead, by contrast (**contrast**); for example, for instance, to illustrate this, in the case of (**illustration**); in the first place/firstly, secondly, finally (**order**); the former, the latter, in this case (**distinction**); likewise, while, in the same way (**parallel**); above all, of great importance (**emphasis**). These functions and examples represent the range of connectives available to the writer: others will occur to you in practice.

PART 3
CONVENTIONS OF FORMAL WRITING

When you are preparing a report many of the items you have to use are written in note-form, and so are points you make yourself in planning the writing of the report. Abbreviation, contraction, dashes and other connecting symbols, numerals, numbering of items in lists – these are the characteristic features of note-form, and their aims are to save the writer time and to provide a clear lay-out of points for ready use in the final draft.

These features, however, are not always appropriate for the final version of the report. The term 'formal continuous prose' is frequently used to describe the style and presentation of a written report. This means writing in the form of connected sentences and paragraphs which obey widely accepted formal conventions. Let us briefly consider these conventions and compare them with some of the features of written notes.

Abbreviation

Two widely used abbreviations in note-form are 'e.g.' ('for example') and 'i.e.' ('that is'). In formal writing the full forms should be used. You should also avoid the common abbreviation 'etc.' – as well as its full form 'etcetera' – in your final draft, useful as it is in notes. An alternative and more acceptable version of 'cars, vans, buses, etc.' might be the use of a general term as in 'cars, vans, buses and other vehicles'. Abbreviations of units of measurement, such as 'km' or 'sec.', are not appropriate in formal continuous prose except in reports of a technical nature when the units are frequently used. This 'rule' applies also to the use of technical terms, which between specialists are often abbreviated but must at least be introduced in full form for the general readership of a report.

On the other hand, there are some abbreviations which *are* conventional in formal writing. Titles, such as 'Mr', 'Mrs', 'Dr' and 'Lt', always retain their short form. Initialled forms and acronyms (R.S.P.C.A. and NATO, for example) are acceptable as long as they are widely known. If in your opinion an organisation is not immediately recognised by its initials then you should use its full form in the first instance and its initials in further mentions.

Contraction

Except in direct quotation, contracted forms such as 'I'm', 'don't', 'there's', 'can't', 'isn't' and 'it's' should not be used in formal writing. Contractions contribute to the effect of an informal or colloquial style since they reproduce conversation.

Numerals

Common sense and consistency of use are the watchwords when you are deciding whether to use figures or words when expressing numbers. In general you should reserve figures for larger numbers and use words for anything under a hundred: for example, write 'seventy-eight people attended the meeting' but 'there is room for 2750 cars'. However, if in your judgment there are too many numerals included in a report for word forms to be comfortable, then you should use figures, as for example when you are dealing with comparative percentages. Dates, monetary amounts and times of the day should be expressed in figures.

If you consider it appropriate to convert exact numbers into approximate amounts, either by rounding up or by rounding down, then you should use words. Remember to indicate this by means of preceding words and phrases such as 'approximately', 'nearly', 'almost', 'over' and 'more than'.

Connective symbols

Dashes are useful in note-making, but they should be kept to a minimum in the final draft since excessive use creates an unwanted dramatic or racy style. In formal writing, dashes are used in pairs for parenthesis (in the same way as brackets or comma pairs) and singly for emphasis or to add an additional point.

Some connective symbols save time in note-making but should be replaced by their full word forms in the report. The most common is the ampersand (&) which should always be written as 'and' in the final draft.

Numbering items in a list

In reading other people's notes and organising your own, you can pick up information more efficiently when data are presented in classified form, particularly in lists of numbered items. 'Point-form' is a way of categorising and sub-categorising items by means of a decimal system (1.3, 4.2.1, and so on). In note-making it is especially useful for organising complex material – see Step Four of the Planning Guide in Practice in Section One of this book for a simple example of this system.

In the formal continuous prose style of a report, however, categorised relationships should usually be expressed completely in words. The use of structural linkage, dealt with in the previous part of this section, is particularly important here. In reports that are much longer than the ones in this book the numbering of sections is of course necessary because of the mass of information facing the reader.

CONCLUDING NOTE

Now that you have been introduced to the skills of planning and writing reports, you should feel confident about making use of these skills in a variety of situations requiring formal communication for practical purposes.

Although we have focused our attention on reports as written accounts for individual or groups of readers, we should remember that reports can be heard as well as read. Indeed, the task in Activity Unit Six was to produce a report that was suitable to be read aloud to a radio audience. Whether reports are intended for readers or listeners they must still be planned and drafted in the same way, even though differences in style and expression may occur. A good report, whatever the nature of its audience – be they readers or listeners – must succeed equally as words in the ear as well as words on the page.

And finally, apart from the sheer practice of composing them, one of the best ways to improve the writing of reports is to read and listen to other people's.

APPENDIX

Glossary of Terms used in Report Writing

Abbreviation
Shortened form of a word by which it can still be identified.

Ambiguity (unintended)
Imprecision of expression occurring when meanings other than the one intended by the writer can be inferred by the reader.

Ampersand
Short symbol for 'and' (&) useful in note-making but unacceptable in formal writing.

Body of Report
The substance of the report, material contained in paragraphs other than the introduction and conclusion.

Checklist (*see*** Planning Checklist)**

Cohesion
The structural arrangement of ideas in sentences and paragraphs so as to form a logical, unified whole.

Colloquial
A term used to describe a written style that is characteristic of informal conversation.

Conclusion
The final paragraph of the report. If appropriate, this is where a recommendation is stated.

Context
As applied to communication, this term is used to identify the circumstances in which language is being used. (*See also* **Report Situation**.)

Continuous Prose
Writing which consists of fully formed sentences which are logically organised into paragraphs.

Contraction
The omission of letters to form either a shortened word or a single word from more than one by the use of the apostrophe.

Conventions
With reference to formal writing, these are the practices which are widely agreed as characteristic of acceptable written expression.

Data
The items of material which are given to the writer as a basis for his or her report.

Direct Speech
The full, verbatim quotation in the written form of what someone has spoken. Double inverted commas (" ... ") are the conventional markers for direct speech.

Ellipsis
Omission of words needed to complete the meaning of a sentence.

Evaluation
The process of judging the relative importance of items of material so as to decide what should be included in, and what should be excluded from, a report. The writer's evaluation is also applied to the 'surviving' items so that some are highlighted or expanded while others are reduced to a summarised form.

Expansion
The development into a more detailed version of an item of material which, in the writer's judgment, requires greater prominence or was originally presented in condensed note-form. (*See* its opposite, **Summary**.)

Exposition
The laying out of the theme of the report, beginning in the introductory paragraph and developing through subsequent paragraphs.

Expression
In writing this applies to words and phrases which carry the writer's meaning to the reader. It is effective when this is done with a minimum of misunderstanding.

Formal
As applied to the tone, or more generally the style, of a report, this refers to writing which is appropriate to the task of conveying information in a serious, straight-forward way. Formal writing is typified by the absence of colloquialisms, slang, jargon or regional dialect.

Grammatical Choice
An aspect of style involving decisions between one or the other correct grammatical form in order to provide the most effective vehicle for what has to be written.

Illustration
The use of examples to clarify a general point.

Indirect Speech (*See* **Reported Speech**)

Informal
In contrast with formal writing, this term describes writing which is conversational in style. It is appropriate when the writer–reader relationship is relaxed and personal.

Information

As applied to report writing tasks, this denotes the data (items of material) offered to the writer together with the requirements, stated purposes and suggested outlines that may be included in the tasks.

Introduction

The opening paragraph of the report, containing in precise form all that is required for the reader to 'tune in' to the topic and purpose with which the writer is concerned. The introduction should also set the tone of the report.

Linkage

An important feature of structural cohesion. It is the use of connective words and phrases so as to signal and reinforce the logical relationships of ideas in a piece of continuous prose.

Notes

A condensed and abbreviated form of writing which makes use of connective symbols and spatial arrangements in order to make clear at a glance the essential information a reader needs. In report planning notes are important in two ways: as a form of presentation of data to be evaluated by the writer, and as a first draft of the material on which the report is to be based.

Objective

A term describing the stance of a report writer in relation to the topic being dealt with. 'Objective' denotes a neutral or impersonal stance and indicates the writer's primary purpose as being to inform the reader rather than, say, to persuade.

Ordering

The sequencing of ideas in a report in accordance with its purpose. Almost always, the writer needs to **reorder** the items of material originally presented.

Overview

The overall idea of the main sections of the report. If the overview is not made clear by an outline of the sections to be dealt with, then the writer must construct one.

Paragraph

A unit of sentences dealing with the same topic, often beginning with a 'topic sentence'. In reports, separate paragraphs usually correspond to the main sections identified in the outline.

Parenthesis

A word or group of words inserted into a sentence which is grammatically complete without it. It enables the writer to add a point or supply an example without interrupting the flow of the main sentence. Parenthesis has three kinds of markers: a pair of brackets, a pair of dashes and a pair of commas.

Passive Voice

A grammatical form expressing an action as something performed *by* an agent, either explicitly when the agent is identified or implicity when he, she or it is not identified. This is in contrast to the **active voice** in which the subject of the verb performs the action.

Planning Checklist

An important stage in the planning of a report during which the writer identifies the topic, his or her expected role, the readership and the purpose – the elements which form the basis of the completed report.

Purpose

The aim of the report, which must be clear to the writer from the start and communicated to the reader from the opening paragraph.

Readership

The person or people for whom the report is intended. The writer's notion of his or her readership helps to determine the selection of content and choice of style (especially tone).

Relevance

This term refers to the question of which of the many items of material with which the report writer is presented are, in the writer's judgment, appropriate for inclusion. The planning checklist will produce the criteria to determine which items are relevant.

Report

A formally written account which is governed by terms of reference known to both writer and readers. It is carefully compiled from data available to the writer and is directed towards achieving a specific purpose.

Report Situation

All that is available to the report writer in the form of instructions, background details, items of material (data) and suggested outline of main sections.

Reported Speech

The indirect but accurate representations of the words of a speaker as though reported by the listener to a third person. In reports this is a useful twofold technique: it allows greater economy than direct speech and it imparts a more formal tone to the content of the original utterance.

Role

The function of the writer in producing a report. Even if the role is not specified in the 'report situation' it may be determined by the combination of topic, readership and purpose.

Selection

The process of choosing from all the available data those points which the report writer judges to be relevant according to the planning checklist.

Structure

The ordering and linking of words and word-groups into wholes. There are two dimensions of structure: internal sentence structure or overall structure.

Style

In language, this refers to the ways in which a person communicating with someone else adapts his or her use of language to the situation in which the language occurs. In report writing it is a formal style that is generally most appropriate, the three elements of which are tone, expression and grammatical choice.

Subjective

A term (distinct from **objective**) describing the stance of a report writer in relation to the topic being dealt with. 'Subjective' describes a personally involved stance on the writer's part, the focus of the report being on his or her opinion. In some cases, the subjective element is restricted to the last section of the report where, for example, a recommendation is expressed.

Summary

A reduced version (or precis) of the original piece of writing containing the gist or main points. Supporting details and illustrative material are normally excluded. (*See* its opposite, **expansion**.)

Terms of Reference

Instructions or guidelines given to the report writer which he or she must adopt as a framework for the report. It is essential that the terms of reference be conveyed accurately to the reader at the outset so that the topic and purpose of the report can be readily understood.

Tone

An aspect of style which, in writing, conveys the writer's attitude to the subject and establishes a particular relationship with the reader. Reports require a formal tone, which is achieved by certain acceptable variations in vocabulary, sentence form and punctuation.

Topic

The subject or theme of the report – what it should be about as distinct from the purpose it must serve.

Verbosity

Wordiness – the use of more words than is necessary or desirable.

Vocabulary

The writer's choice of words. The vocabulary of a report should be appropriate to its topic, readership and purpose and should contribute to a formal style.

Acknowledgements

The author and publisher are grateful to the following for permission to reproduce extracts from their publications:

Industrial Tribunals Procedure, HMSO pamphlet 1987: p. 21; *Unfairly Dismissed*, HMSO pamphlet, 1986: p. 21; *Evening News*, Edinburgh, 26/11/88; *The Sweet Life* (adapted): p. 24; *Inform*, Home and Law Publishing Ltd: p. 25; Anne Barnett, *Food and Nutrition for You*, Hutchinson, 1985: p. 26; Patty Fisher & Arnold Bender, *The Value of Food*, (2nd edn), Oxford University Press, 1975: pp. 26–7; *Practical Ways to Crack Crime*, HMSO, 1988: pp. 41–2, 44–5, 47; *Police Advice: Don't Let Them Get Away With It*, HMSO, leaflet, 1985: pp. 42–3; *Knock, Knock, Who's There?* HMSO leaflet, 1988: p. 43.

The publishers have made every effort to trace the copyright holders, but if they have inadvertently overlooked any they will be pleased to make the necessary arrangements at the first opportunity.